WITHOUT SAYING A WORD

Master the Science of Body Language and Maximize Your Success

KASIA WEZOWSKI

AND

PATRYK WEZOWSKI

HarperCollins
LEADERSHIP
AN IMPRINT OF HarperCollins

Published by HarperCollins Leadership, an imprint of HarperCollins.

Drawings by Magdalena Dabrowska.

Book design by Elyse Strongin, Neuwirth & Associates.

ISBN 978-0-8144-3974-6 (eBook)

Library of Congress Cataloging-in-Publication Data

Names: Wezowski, Kasia, author. | Wezowski, Patryk, author. | Wezowski, Patryk. Lichaamstaal. English
Title: Without saying a word : master the science of body language and maximize your success / Kasia Wezowski and Patryk Wezowski.
Description: New York : American Management Association, [2018] | Originally published in Dutch in 2013 as Lichaamstaal by Patryk Wezowski & Kasia Wezowski | Includes bibliographical references and index.
Identifiers: LCCN 2018003567 (print) | LCCN 2018005276 (ebook) | ISBN 9780814439746 (ebook) | ISBN 9780814439739 (pbk.)
Subjects: LCSH: Body language. | Success.
Classification: LCC BF637.N66 (ebook) | LCC BF637.N66 W49 2018 (print) | DDC 302.2/22—dc23
LC record available at https://lccn.loc.gov/2018003567

ISBN 978-0-8144-3973-9

Printed in the United States of America

18   19   20   21   22   LSC   10   9   8   7   6   5   4   3   2   1

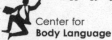

Center for
Body Language

www.CenterForBodyLanguage.com

WITHOUT SAYING A WORD

Contents

Acknowledgments   **vii**

Introduction   **1**

1. The Five Principles of Body Language Intelligence   **15**

2. Self-confident Body Language   **25**

3. Positive Body Language   **49**

4. Negative Body Language   **85**

5. How Body Language Reveals Emotions   **119**

6. Interpreting Facial Expressions   **145**

7. Microexpressions: The Dead Giveaways   **175**

8. Decisionmaking Body Language   **191**

9. Practice Exercises   **219**

Bibliography   **231**

Index   **239**

Acknowledgments

The knowledge contained in this book is the result of more than two decades of passion for body language and many years of training in the field of nonverbal communication, in the course of which we received much valuable feedback from many thousands of participants. We are most grateful to our certified trainers who have carried out excellent work worldwide on behalf of the Centre for Body Language.

We would like thank our long-term partners around the world: Antonio Sacavem and Ana Sacavem (Portugal), Husam Al-Eid (MENA Region), Jose Manuel Jimenez and Baldiri Pons (Spain), Leopoldo Uprimny (Columbia), Laura Justicia (Argentina), Juan Carlos Garcia (Panama), Caroline Matteucci (Switzerland), Serkan Tunc (Turkey), Muhammad Ali (Pakistan), Roberto Micarelli (Italy), Eddy Vandeweyer, Jazz Jagarnathsingh (the Netherlands), Dana Ketels, Sofie-Ann Bracke (Belgium), and Mills Wong (Hong Kong). We are similarly grateful to over a thousand other trainers from around the world, who use our methodology and have thereby contributed over the years to the wider dissemination of our approach to body language.

Friends who provided us with interesting ideas, partners and course participants who gave us valuable feedback, and other people to whom we owe a debt of gratitude for their willingness to spread the ideas of the Centre for Body Language include Nancy De Bonte, An Declercq, Peter Saerens, Ann Van Den Begin, Annemie Janssens, Céline de Crombrugghe, Michael Cianchetti, Don Wells, Geert Van de Velde, Karolina Szczepankowska, Magdalena Dabrowska, Saskia Smet, Marie-Rose Mens, Patrick Adler, Susan Ockers, Kevin de Smet, Jean-Louis de Hasque, Tom Coreynen, Tom Van Diest, Dirk Vermant, Robin Vissenaekens, Hilde Vernaillen, Matt Roosen, Carine Cappelle, Guido Poffé, Roland Duchatelet, Wim Hoeckman, Bart Van Coppenolle, Karl Raats, Roy Martina, Pascale Van Damme, Robin Vissenaekens, Emmanuel Mottrie, Gina De Groote, Bart Loos, Guy Vereecke, Frietjhof Croon, Walter Van Gorp, Eric de Vries, Jos Theunissen, Johan Spruyt, Richard Barrett, Bruno Desmet, Wim Hoeckman, Greg S. Reid, Glenna Trout, Dirk Vermant, Roland Duchatelet, and Alan Cohen.

The scientific and academic information contained in the book is the result of more than 150 years of research into body language. Huge contributions to the generation and interpretation of this accumulated wisdom have been made by numerous professors and scientists, many of whom have influenced the content of the following pages. Consequently, we wish to express our heartfelt thanks to Duchenne De Boulogne, Charles Darwin, Robert Plutchik, Carroll Izard, Robert Rosenthal, Chris Kleinke, Robert

Goldberg, Edward Hall, Gerard Nierenberg, Henry Calero, Desmond Morris, Paul Ekman, Wallace Friesen, Alan Pease, Ekhard Hess, Mark Knapp, Judee Burgoon, Michael Argyle, Dan O'Hair, Barry Schlenker, and Ralph Exline.

Last but not least, we would also like to thank our many associates and colleagues, whose willingness to exchange ideas and information about body language and nonverbal communication has had a significant impact on our activities over the years. These include Carol Kinsey Goman, Mark Bowden, Beverly Flaxington, Renate Mousseux, Ian Trudel, Elizabeth Kuhnke, Mark McClish, Dominika Maison, Robert Phipps, Greg Williams, Henrik Fexeus, Joe Navarro, and Rick Kirschner.

WITHOUT SAYING A WORD

Introduction

Your Body Language Intelligence Determines Your Success

Several years ago, Patryk and I were invited to predict the results of a startup pitch contest in Vienna, where 2,500 tech entrepreneurs were competing. We observed the presentations, but rather than paying attention to the ideas the entrepreneurs pitched, we watched the body language and microexpressions of the judges as they listened. We gave our predictions of who would win before the winners were announced; as we and the audience soon learned, we were spot on. We had spoiled the surprise.

Two years later we were invited back to the same event. This time, instead of watching the judges, we observed the contestants. Our task was not to guess the winners, but to determine how presenters' nonverbal communication contributed to their success or failure.

We evaluated each would-be entrepreneur on a scale from 0 to 15. People scored points for each sign of positive, confident body language, such as smiling, maintaining eye contact, and persuasive gesturing. They lost points for each negative signal, such as fidgeting, stiff hand movements, and averted eyes.

We found that contestants whose pitches were rated in the top eight by competition judges scored an average of 8.3 on our fifteen-point scale, while those who did not place in that top tier had an average score of 5.5. Positive body language strongly correlated with more successful outcomes.

We've found similar correlations in the political realm. Let's look at the last two U.S. presidential elections.

During the 2012 campaign, we conducted an online study in which a thousand participants—both Democrats and Republicans—watched two-minute video clips featuring Barack Obama and Mitt Romney at campaign events delivering both neutral and emotional content.

Webcams recorded the viewers' facial expressions, and our team analyzed them for six key emotional responses identified in psychology research: happy, surprised, afraid, disgusted, angry, and sad. We coded for the tenor of the emotion (positive or negative) and how strongly it seemed to be expressed. This analysis showed that Obama sparked stronger emotional responses and fewer negative ones. Even a significant number of Republicans—16 percent—reacted negatively to Romney.

When we analyzed the candidates' body language, we found that Obama's resembled those of our pitch contest winners. He displayed primarily open, positive, confident positions congruent with his speech. Romney, by contrast, often gave out negative signals, diminishing his message with contradictory and distracting facial expressions and movement.

The 2016 presidential election also revealed a stark contrast between the body language of the two candidates, which was noticeable throughout the debates. While Obama was able to gain an advantage over Romney in part because of his more convincing nonverbal communication, in the 2016 election neither Clinton nor Trump was able to use body language to create a positive impression.

Trump's hypermasculine behavior and his disconcerting habit of following Clinton on stage as she talked was highly off-putting to many viewers and voters. Clinton was more controlled than Trump, but perhaps too much so. She was widely seen as inauthentic; her studied mannerisms, in fact, made it harder for the audience to connect with her.

Neither Clinton nor Trump's debate performance was bad enough to alienate their core audiences. A large number of people responded well to Clinton's composure; likewise, other people liked Trump's brash swagger. However, if one of the candidates had been able to behave a bit more like Obama and form an authentic connection with voters outside their normal base, it may have improved their chances by widening their appeal.

Of course, the elections didn't hinge on body language! Nor did the results of the startup competition. But the right kinds of nonverbal communication do correlate with success.

Great Communicators Read Body Language

Although most of us like to think of ourselves as rational decisionmakers, ample research shows that emotions play an outsized role in sales and negotiations. If you can't read what your counterpart is feeling and instead focus only on what she is saying, you're highly unlikely to achieve everything you could have.

Of course, experienced negotiators know how to mask their true feelings. They choose their words, tone, body language, and expressions carefully. To the average observer, they often appear neutral, impassive. Or they're able to convincingly fake an emotion if they think it will help them advance their own interests.

However, there is a way to read what your counterpart is feeling even if they are deliberately trying to hide it from you. The secret is to pay attention to the spontaneous and involuntary microexpressions that rapidly flit across everyone's faces at times of intense emotion. If you know what to look for, microexpressions can provide an instant, honest window into how your counterpart is feeling.

In our work in body language research and instruction, we've long theorized that one of the key differences between exceptional negotiators or salespeople and those who are merely average is the ability to read these microexpressions. This enables them to gauge visceral reactions to ideas or proposals, and then strategically steer the other person toward a preferred outcome.

To test this idea, we conducted two experiments using videos that measure users' ability to recognize these expressions.

In the first study, we compared the video test scores of salespeople from the Myo Company with their performances and found that those with above-average scores noticeably outsold their colleagues. The second experiment involved salespeople from a BMW showroom in Rome, Italy. We found that high performers (who had sold more than sixty automobiles in the most recent quarter) scored almost twice as high on the test as low performers. Our conclusion: Effective negotiators seem to be naturally good at reading microexpressions.

Anyone Can Increase Their Body Language Intelligence

Body language intelligence is closely correlated with professional success and general happiness. Projecting confident, trustworthy body language enhances the impact of your presentations. The ability to read body language and microexpressions increases your skill as a negotiator and salesperson. Studying body language increases your *emotional intelligence*, which enhances the quality of all of your relationships.

Some people are born with a natural gift for body language, but anyone can learn to increase their body language intelligence through study and practice.

Six years ago, we were asked to develop a training course for call centers. The participants in the course only had contact with their customers by telephone. You might think that the call center operatives could best learn to interact better with customers by learning the right set of "formulas": how to deliver the appropriate sales pitch in the appropriate manner to land bigger orders or to soothe difficult clients.

After a number of the course participants gave a demonstration of how they handle their telephone conversations, we told them that our training would not focus on learning set formulas or on correct voice intonation. Instead, we wanted them to concentrate on the body language of the people giving the demonstrations. In particular, we asked what they could deduce from the posture and attitude of these demonstrators. It soon became clear that body language could have a major influence on the resulting conversations.

One of the participants sat in a very uncomfortable position and had a furrowed brow while she talked to customers. As a result, she sounded irritated. Another leaned back in his chair with his legs wide open. His face had a superior look, which was reflected by the arrogant tone in his voice. This made his conversation partner—the customer on the other end of the line—less willing to answer his questions.

A third participant was hunched up in a posture that betrayed insecurity—which was plain to hear in the way she spoke. A fourth person flicked through his manual of sales formulas while conducting his conversation. He sounded distracted and failed to concentrate on what he was saying and hearing, which made his conversation partner feel ignored and unimportant.

What is striking about these different approaches is that all the participants were following exactly the same conversation plan and speaking exactly the same words, which they had all learned by heart. However, their body language had a big impact on the way they actually spoke, which in turn had a big impact on the way their conversation partners experienced hearing them.

We realized from these observations that it was more important for us to concentrate on body language and on changing the participants' work posture/attitude, than on trying to alter their voices or the content of the words. It also soon became clear that some of the trainees were transferring their own bad moods to the people they were talking to. This negative approach may have been carried over from the way they felt at home, or it may have been the result of some personal conviction, or it may simply have been caused by something that had irritated the participant earlier in the day. Whatever the reason, their body language during their telephone conversations with their customers spoke volumes about what they were really feeling inside. Just as crucially, their nonverbal behavior had a powerful influence on their customers, who in turn became nervous, irritated, or arrogant. This confirmed what we already knew: Body language shows what is happening inside your body and mind. If you want to change that body language, the only way to do it is to start with your own emotions and moods.

❝ Your body always wants to tell the truth about what you are feeling. ❞

THE TRUTH ABOUT BODY LANGUAGE

A good knowledge of body language helps you to be more aware of what someone else is really feeling. It is therefore the ideal compass for every conversation. The nonverbal signals that we transmit with our bodies are the signposts that can lead us along the right road to successful communication. However, an understanding of body language alone cannot change the underlying emotions it reflects.

Body language is a kind of stethoscope: It helps you to examine the possible causes of certain types of behavior from the outside. However, it cannot change what is happening on the inside without help.

When you are aware of certain emotions, it becomes easier to focus on them and transform them. But trying to adjust your body language without changing something inside is counterproductive. The nonverbal signals you send out are not controllable: Your body will always want to tell the truth about what you are feeling.

Take, for example, someone who is nervous before giving a presentation. Even though she tries hard to adopt all the self-confident attitudes and poses outlined in Chapter 3, if she does not feel genuinely calm inside there will always be something that escapes her attention or comes across to others as fake. Changing your body language without thinking about your underlying emotions is pointless. Body language allows us to quickly and accurately identify our internal emotions and their influence on our behavior. These internal emotions need to be transformed before we can expect to see any external improvement in our body language. The tips and exercises in this book make this change possible—almost overnight.

Changing Your Body Language

The training for the call center operatives began with relaxation exercises to help improve their general mood. Many participants took our advice to participate in sports between training sessions and to devote more time to things they liked doing. One of them began coming to work on his motorcycle. Another went swimming two or three times a week. Some decided to spend more quality time with their families. Others got into meditation or mindfulness.

The aim was to relax the tension in their muscles, since that tension made their voices sound stiff and cool when speaking on the phone. A secondary objective was to make them aware that their work took up the largest part of their day so it was worth making an effort to make that work more pleasant, regardless of whether they did the job because they liked it or because it was just a way to pay the bills. Instead of being irritated and frustrated for forty hours a week, impatiently waiting for the weekend to come, surely it was better to feel relaxed at work, laughing with your colleagues, and showing more understanding for your customers? This was the core of our message.

Each group had six days of training divided into three cycles. We also worked on the participants' verbal communication, but we always related it to a conscious awareness of their body language. This not only gave participants greater insight into the best strategies to use with their customers, but also gave them a more positive attitude toward their work. One of the company directors commented afterward that it was almost like getting a completely new set of employees, so great was the change in their voices and their styles of communication.

All the transformations were realized at the level of the participants' body language, which promoted better contact with their customers. Why? Because your body language expresses your emotions, and this language is more important than the language of mere words. People not only react to what you say, but to what you do and the way you do it. In other words, to your body language.

BODY LANGUAGE EXPERTS AND MARITAL SECRETS

Participants in our courses often ask if it's difficult for two body language experts to be married to each other. Is it irritating to see what the other is thinking or feeling without even saying a word?

The short answer is no. We have no secrets from each other and feel the need for none. We both believe that authenticity and honesty are the best approach to any relationship. We regard it as a kind of added value that we are so quickly able to assess each other's feelings. This results in a tighter bond, fewer misunderstandings, greater trust, and more empathy for each other. Body language deepens friendships and relationships. The only difficult thing is that we sometimes find it hard to surprise each other: Body language never lies.

What's more, body language can accelerate the "getting-to-know-you" process at the beginning of a relationship. A sharp and intuitive sense for body language signals can help you to feel whether or not someone might be a suitable partner. Over the years we have lost many "friends" as a result of our expertise in nonverbal communication. But the friends we have retained are true and genuine friends, on whom we know we can rely.

After you have read this book, you may come to the conclusion that your partner is no longer as crazy about you as you once thought, or that your boss will never give that promotion you so desperately want, or that your best friend is clearly keeping something hidden from you. If that's the way things are, so be it. We have never seen the value of prolonging an artificial relationship any longer than is necessary. Open, honest, and transparent communication is always the best policy. In the long term, this is the only way to ensure that a marriage is a happy one. So, are you ready to start your own personal journey to authenticity? Because once you have read this book, there will be no turning back.

How Scientifically Valid Are Interpretations of Body Language?

There has been a long dispute between those who claim that the interpretation of body language is grounded in science and those who argue that it is unscientific. We would like to use the following example to clarify our position: What is yawning? For many years, it was thought that the purpose of yawning was to bring more air into the body when it was in short supply. However, in 2002 Mark A. W. Andrews published a paper in which he argued that this theory was incorrect, since the lungs are not independently capable of recognizing a lower level of oxygen in the bodily system. In 2007, Andrew C. Gallup and Gordon G. Gallup investigated whether or not yawning might serve to lower the temperature of the brain. At the International Conference on Yawning it was announced that yawning is an expression of arousal. Since then, several other researchers have given different explanations. In other words, even an easily identifiable and seemingly simple bodily action like yawning has no universally accepted interpretation.

Similarly, correct interpretation of body language is primarily dependent on knowledge of and your experience with the phenomenon. Our interpretations are based on the most current scientific studies. But the science of body language is living science: Every day new and fascinating discoveries are being made about the way the human body works. As you will see, some interpretations are culture dependent. Other aspects are driven by human evolution, and therefore learned by us all from an early age, or else are observable in a similar form in nature.

The focus of this book is to provide straightforward, clear, and usable guidelines to people who want to apply the science of nonverbal communication in everyday conversations. The book should also satisfy those who prefer to see the scientific evidence on which our guidelines are based, particularly in the sections dealing with microexpressions, the eyes, and the smile. For further study, you can also check our source material using the bibliography at the end of the book.

" How can I apply the science of body language in my everyday conversations? "

According to the British biologist Desmond Morris, people communicate with more than 3,000 different gestures. The gestures that are discussed in the following pages are mainly those found in business conversations and are relatively easy to interpret. More complex emotional experiences, such as shyness or pain, require greater expertise to interpret, and are beyond the scope of this book. Shyness and pain can be displayed by more than ten different signals or combination of signals. At the same time, it is very difficult to distinguish between a real and a pretended experience of these sensations.

In much the same way, we chose not to discuss in detail the signals that cause the most controversy among scientists (for example, whether or not a sudden fright reaction, such as might be caused by an explosion, can be described as an emotion). While fascinating, these discussions would take space away from the true focus of the book: How can I apply the science of body language in my everyday conversations?

To draw the most accurate conclusions, it is first necessary to learn about five basic principles for the interpretation of body language. (This is the subject of Chapter 1.) These principles help you to choose the right explanation for a particular visual cue. One of the more innovative aspects of the book is the division into seven groups of the most useful, most usable, and most common nonverbal signals that occur in everyday conversation.

Chapter 2 deals with gestures that support contact with other people. These postures and attitudes often have a positive effect on the conversation; as a result, we generally refer to them as "positive body language."

Chapter 3 looks at movements that exude self-confidence and dominance. Behavior that is too dominant or leads to breaking off contact is examined in Chapter 4 as "negative body language."

All body language reflects emotions that are being experienced, but in Chapter 5 we will explore in particular forms of nonverbal communication that primarily indicate the intense experience of various emotions.

Emotions that can be communicated by the face form the basis for Chapter 6.

In Chapter 7, we will take a closer look at microexpressions, a special form of short and subtle facial expressions.

Chapter 8 is devoted to expressions and gestures that are useful in negotiations, because they reflect the body language that is relevant to the decisionmaking process.

In Chapter 9, you can apply (using the SCAN method) what you have learned about body language to a number of standard situations in which expressions and gestures from all the chapters are included.

At the end of each chapter, there is a clear and simple summary. This will help you to apply your growing knowledge of body language during day-to-day conversations, sales pitches, interviews, and negotiations. In addition to teaching you how to interpret body language, our book aims to go a step further: Once you understand the meaning of certain manifestations of body language, what do you do with this information? How do you react? To help you answer these questions, most of the gestures and expressions are accompanied by useful tips about the best way to respond if your conversation partners display this type of behavior. In this way, you will be able to achieve your conversational objective in the quickest and easier manner.

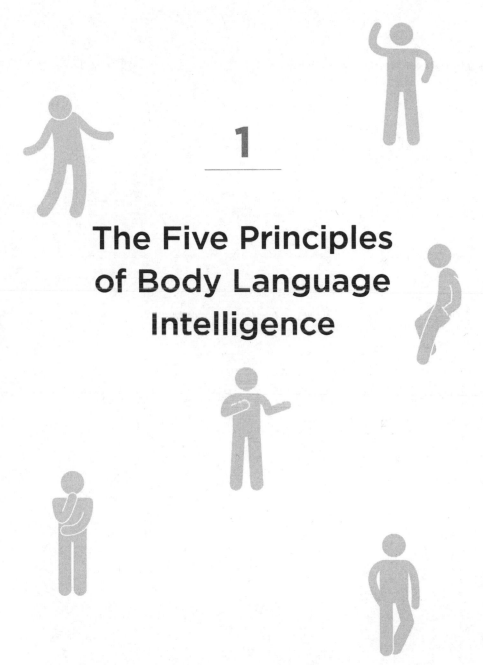

1

The Five Principles of Body Language Intelligence

For every interpretation of body language, it is important to devote attention to a number of crucial principles that influence the meaning of all attitudes, gestures, and expressions (and also the conclusions you draw about them). These five principles are the bedrock of meaningful body language interpretation. You'll learn to increase your body language intelligence by connecting what you see on the outside to what is really happening on the inside.

These basic principles apply to nonverbal communication in photographs and films, as well as in conversations. Learning to take proper account of all five basic principles when you interpret body language and apply them to your conclusions is the foundation of correctly understanding what's *really* being communicated in your daily interactions.

1. Combinations Confirm Your Assumptions

The interpretations that you will find in the following chapters are only accurate in 60 to 80 percent of situations, if they occur singly or in isolation. If you see a certain movement occur repeatedly, the likelihood is greater that the interpretation is correct. If within a short period of time you see a combination of three to five movements that all give a similar signal, you can draw your conclusion with a high degree of certainty.

If someone touches the tip of his nose just once during a conversation, it may be that he simply has an itchy nose. But if during a two-minute period someone touches his nose, rubs his eyes, covers his mouth, takes a step backward, avoids eye contact, and crosses his arms, then there is a good chance that he either finds the situation stressful or that he is lying.

2. What Is Happening on the Inside Is What You See on the Outside

If you have to make a choice between what you hear (words) and what you see (movements), it is better to believe what you see. The body compensates for the things that are said. It is possible to put up a pretense or to hide stress for a short time, but as far as nonverbal communication is concerned it is much more difficult to conceal or falsify crucial information. Why? Our body instinctively shows on the outside what is happening on the inside.

Numerous studies have shown that our limbic system works faster than our powers of rational thought; expressions and gestures tend to tell the truth before we can consciously adjust our behavior. This conscious adjustment is ten thousand times slower than the uncontrollable signals of the limbic system. What people are experiencing internally will therefore be visible externally. The reverse is true as well: When you see someone with a facial expression that is not sad, it is highly likely that this person is not experiencing sadness at that moment. However, you still need to take into account principle number 5: If this person never has a sad facial expression, even at times when you know that she is experiencing sadness, you will need to amend your conclusions.

3. Context Influences Body Language

During our training courses, we are often asked: If someone often crosses his arms, does this mean he has a closed personality? What do you think? Is the answer to this question yes or no? If you correctly apply basic principle number 3, the right answer is "it all depends." Whether or not someone has her arms crossed is dependent on the context in which she finds herself. For example, a person standing outside in the middle of winter who has forgotten her coat may very well have her arms crossed, but this simply means that she is cold. At the same time, she may very well be conducting a pleasant and enthusiastic conversation with her friends!

But what about someone dressed in doctor's clothing and discussing something with a colleague in a hospital corridor? Hospitals are usually warm, so that in this case the crossed arms probably have something to do with the nature of the conversation. In other words, you need to pay careful attention to the location, the situation, and the surroundings of the person about whom you wish to draw conclusions.

❝ Body language always compensates for the things that are said with words. ❞

4. Look for Changes

We always try to avoid making interpretations based on a single photograph. If you have no points of comparison, your conclusions will be less accurate. To make reliable conclusions, what we look for above all are large and strong changes in body language positions. For example, if someone suddenly puts his legs in a debate position during a negotiation, while he otherwise seems relaxed, this has much greater meaning than if he has his legs in the debate position from the beginning of the discussion.

Timing is also very important: A significant change in body language position at the moment when a new price is mentioned says much more than if the same movement is made at a neutral moment in the conversation.

5. Take Account of Habits

When we give interpretations of meaning for a gesture like touching your nose, we often hear people say: "Yes, but I regularly touch the end of my nose when I am speaking. Everyone in my family does it. But it doesn't mean we are lying!" This may be true: When you apply the fifth basic principle touching the nose may lose its traditional interpretation. Pay careful attention to the habits of the person you are interpreting as well as to movements that are "normal" for someone in the specific situation.

If someone has developed a particular movement as a habit over a number of years, normal interpretations of this movement given in the following chapters will not necessarily be correct.

If, for instance, someone is always in the habit of smiling, even when she is feeling hostile, then you cannot automatically interpret this person's smile as an indication of pleasure. In order to know which movements, gestures, and expressions you need to exclude from your interpretation as unreliable, you first need to examine a sufficient number of situations to establish this person's habits. In addition to habits, outside factors such as taking drugs or medicines, using alcohol, or having gesture altering treatments such as plastic surgery or Botox can all play a role. By taking proper account of a person's habits, you can avoid mistakes such as interpreting a genuine expression of pleasure as an expression of contempt.

" Everybody speaks a body language. "

IS BODY LANGUAGE CULTURE DEPENDENT?

Experts are divided on this question. It is a subject that can lead to endless discussions, not least because of the need to first define exactly what is meant by the terms "body language" and "culture dependent" in the context of this specific question.

For example, some gestures are extremely offensive in one country, but very positive elsewhere. Consider the "circle" gesture made by closing the thumb and the index finger. In the United States and countries like Belgium and the Netherlands, this means "okay." In France, it means "zero." In Brazil, it means . . . something you should probably avoid saying. In this case, body language clearly differs from culture to culture. However, there are certain microexpressions that studies have shown to be associated with particular emotions in the same way in more than twenty different cultures. Similarly, North Americans and Europeans will make some hand gestures less frequently but bigger, whereas Asians will make the same gesture more frequently but smaller. Does this mean that in these contexts body language is culture independent?

So, which of the experts are right? It is difficult to say, but these examples make clear that the subject of nonverbal communication is not only wide-ranging and complex, but also depends on how you interpret the term "body language." One thing is certain: One way or another, everybody speaks a body language.

The five basic principles are crucial. To draw accurate conclusions, you must apply all five to every interpretation of body language you make. Always keep them in mind and test all your assumptions against them. To make them easy to remember, we have combined the most important word of each of the five principles into the following sentence:

"Combinations Within Context Change Habits."

With these five basic principles for interpreting body language, you are sufficiently well-armed to correctly identify the meanings of the movements, gestures, and expressions in the following chapters.

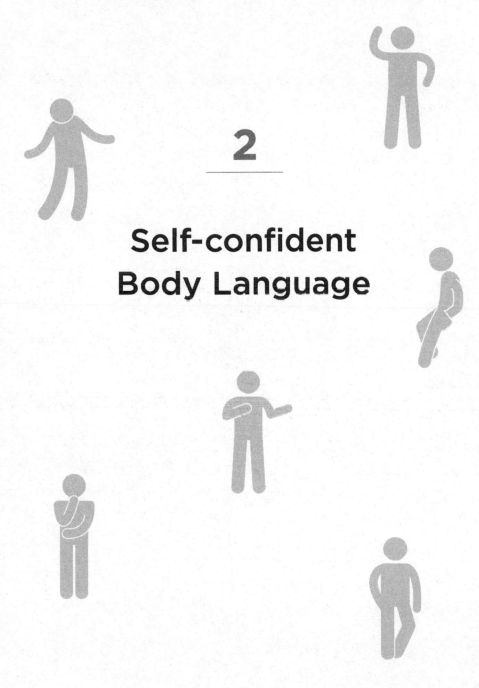

2

Self-confident
Body Language

IN THIS CHAPTER, YOU'LL DISCOVER:

- How to recognize when your conversation partner is receptive
- The body movements that stimulate trust and cooperation

When I was thirteen years old, my first job was to distribute fliers to pharmacies. This involved me asking the pharmacist if I could place the fliers in a spot where they could easily be seen. Initially, I was very successful. On the first morning, I visited fifteen shops and none of them refused my request. Things went less smoothly for my girlfriend, who had the same task: It took her much longer and some of the pharmacists were unwilling to cooperate.

When it was my turn to be confronted with my first refusal, however, I immediately had the feeling that my initial enthusiasm had disappeared. The energy and power with which I had previously entered the stores were suddenly missing. This change of attitude also had a dramatic impact on my effectiveness. More refusals followed. But what had actually changed? Why did the same sentence—"Can I please put these fliers here on your counter?"—now produce such a different result from a few hours earlier? Why did the change in the way I felt make such a difference to the results I achieved?

What I didn't realize at the time is that the key to success in situations of this kind is not the sentence, but the number of contact-supporting gestures you use when speaking it. The purpose of this chapter is to show you how you can use positive body language to help you convince people and how you can recognize the same signals in others.

Leaning the Upper Body Forward

POSITIVE ATTITUDE, INTEREST

The position of the upper body gives you basic information about the other person's attitude toward you. If the upper body is leaning back or turned away, particularly if the arms are crossed, there is a good chance that the person wants to distance himself from the subject under discussion. Averting the upper body in this way is usually a sign that someone is not listening closely to what you are saying. Perhaps the subject is not important or interesting enough for him to lean forward in your direction. Many studies support this conclusion, including Schlenker in 1975.

If you want someone to listen to you carefully, it is important to get her to orientate her body toward you rather than away from you, since this means interest. You can also try to lean more forward in her direction, since it is possible that the other person may be copying your own more distanced body language. If the other person leans forward at the same moment you do, this is a good sign, because your conversation partner is responding to your positive body language.

Opening the Palms of the Hand

Open palms are a sign of peaceful intentions. It shows that you have nothing to hide, you're unarmed, and you're mentally open to what the other person is saying.

You know that the contact is going well if you regularly see opened palms. This is a sign of openness and a signal to the other person that his words are being experienced as respectful, positive, and valuable. The more frequently a person stretches out his hands in front of him, the greater the openness and honesty he wishes to communicate. This gesture can be strengthened by spreading the fingers or bending them slightly upward, so that the hand forms a kind of cup. Communicating with opened palms improves interpersonal contact. A person whose palms are open is more easily trusted. By showing the inside of our hands, we prove that we have nothing to hide. Liars are more inclined to keep their hands concealed.

There is an historical explanation for the positive meaning attached to open hands. In the past, showing your hands in this way demonstrated that

OPENNESS, HONESTY

you were unarmed and had positive intentions. For this reason, open palms have been associated since ancient times with sincerity, loyalty, and willingness to listen. The signal of surrender—with the hands raised above the head—similarly shows that you do not have a weapon.

This also explains why at crucial moments religious leaders show their palms. Likewise, oaths are often taken with one hand on the heart and the other raised in an open position. This is still the case, for example, when people need to swear on the Bible during legal hearings in court.

If a person intends to be completely open and honest, she will stretch out one or both hands toward her conversation partner. If she wishes to emphasize this gesture, she will show more of the inside of her opened palm. These movements often happen wholly involuntarily, as is the case with so much of body language. When somebody is a bad liar or is trying to hide something, she will often keep her hands held behind her back. In the past, this was also a way to conceal a weapon.

Showing Your Wrists

Women who feel attracted to a man will often hold their glass in a way that exposes their wrists. This can be interpreted as a sign

of openness. In other situations, it means that someone wants to emphasize their sincerity and benign intentions.

OPENNESS, SINCERITY

Hand Movements Near the Mouth

When someone sitting down holds his hands near his mouth and makes gestures that emphasize or support his words, this helps

to ensure a good contact with his conversation partner. Holding the hands in this way emphasizes that the speaker wants to be properly understood, as though he wants to use his hands to give his words more power.

EMPHASIZING WORDS

Open Hands on the Table

If during a negotiation someone pushes her glass or cup to one side—the same side as the hand she was drinking with—this is a sign of openness and acceptance. In this way, her arm movement

OPENNESS, ACCEPTANCE

shows that she wishes to place no barriers between herself and her conversation partner, in contrast to the impression that would be given by moving the cup or glass to the opposite side.

Talking with Your Hands

Some people have the art of being able to talk with their hands. Even if they are speaking to you in a different language, you can still understand what they mean. If you work in the training or sales sectors, talking with your hands can help your listeners to visualize what you are saying. This stimulates the right side of their brains,

ILLUSTRATING WORDS

which processes visualizations, emotions, and intuition. In this way, you communicate with both the rational left half of the brain and with the more emotional right half, which not only makes it easier for listeners to remember new content, but also makes that content seem more convincing. Research by Zuckerman, De Paulo, and Rosenthal in 1981 has shown that liars are less inclined to support their words with their hands.

The Vertical Handshake

In Roman times, it was the custom when shaking hands to grab hold of the other person's wrist. This was a quick way to check that he was not hiding a dagger in his sleeve. Nowadays, a handshake shows that we are willing to make someone's acquaintance. It is an important element in the physical assessment of the other person's energy and vitality. Even in these days of teleconferencing, businesspeople are still prepared to pay the price of an airline ticket so that they can meet future partners face to face and can feel their handshakes. In the Middle East, a written contract is not binding until the two parties have shaken hands.

There are two aspects essential to establish a good and equal understanding during the handshake. First, it is important that both hands are in a vertical position, so that neither of the parties is superior or inferior to the other. Second, the level of pressure applied during the handshake must be the same on both sides. If one person squeezes with 70 percent force, while the other only squeezes with 50 percent, the first person should reduce his pressure by 20 percent. If the other person squeezes with 90 percent force, the first person should increase their pressure by 20 percent until it also comes up to the same level as their partner.

The person who takes the initiative to strengthen or weaken the handshake will depend on the context, the situation, and their awareness of the rules of body language. If you meet a group of ten different people, it is possible that you may also need to change the verticality and the pressure of your handshake ten times, so that you can make everyone's acquaintance on the same footing.

When a man is being introduced to a woman, he may need to adjust handshake pressure and apply relatively less than he would with a man, which is a sign of respect. A man with a positive attitude toward a woman will often automatically reduce his handshake to her level of pressure. A painfully hard handshake might be interpreted by her as a signal of dominance, lack of respect, bad manners, or lack of

EQUALITY, GOOD UNDERSTANDING

empathy. Women should interpret hard handshakes as warn-ings to be careful when dealing with this type of man, since it is possible that he might not fully respect their opinions.

The message for men is that they need to take account of the strength of their hands. Thanks to evolutionary development, the male grip is now capable of exerting a squeezing pressure of forty-five kilograms. In the past, this was useful for carrying, holding, hitting, or throwing things, but power of this kind is less useful in a handshake! We all remember when the newly elected Donald Trump and Emmanuel Macron looked as if they were attempting to squeeze each other to death with their handshakes at the 2017 NATO conference in Brussels. This may make good TV, but it's not a good body language habit to get into.

The Handshake with Both Hands

A handshake with both hands—the so-called glove handshake—can be an expression of warmth, trust, and kindness toward the person whose hand you are shaking. Once again, it is necessary to remember two important aspects.

First, it is the initial positioning of the left hand that makes clear to the other person that you intend to give her a hand-shake with both hands. The movement demonstrates a desire for a sincere relationship, almost as if you wish to embrace her. The left hand serves as the indicator of closeness. The higher you place your left hand on the other person's right arm, the clearer you make your desire to get closer to her in your relationship. It is an expression of your good intentions. Taking hold of the elbow with your left hand demonstrates more affection than taking hold

TRUST, WARM FEELINGS

of the wrist. But don't forget that it is also important to combine these movements with other re-assuring signals, so that the other person does not mistakenly think that the handshake is intended to dominate her.

Second, as the initiating person you need to be aware of how far your left hand intrudes into the other person's personal space. Taking hold of the wrist or the upper arm will only support the contact if a good bond already exists between you. Placing the left hand on the upper arm illustrates a very close level of attachment and is almost equivalent to an embrace. If this warmth of feeling is not mutual or if there is no good reason for the initiator to demonstrate such warmth, the glove handshake may arouse suspicion or even distrust in the other person. It is therefore crucial with this type of handshake to be guided by authentic motives and not simply be a desire to make a good impression.

Stretching Out Your Legs

If the participants in our training sessions stretch out their legs in front of them in a relaxed manner when they are examining the results of one

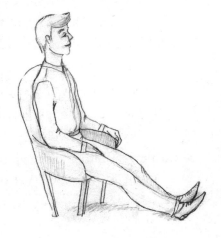

INTEREST, ACCEPTANCE

of the test exercises, this generally means that they found the test interesting. Likewise, if during a discussion one of the conversation partners suddenly uncrosses his legs and stretches them out, this too is a signal of interest and acceptance. If the other conversation partner wishes to express similar interest, she can reciprocate with the same leg movement.

Tilting Your Head to One Side

VULNERABILITY, INTEREST, UNDERSTANDING

Tilting your head to one side is a movement that has its origin in the animal world. An attacking tiger will aim for the neck of its intended victim, since this is the prey's most vulnerable spot. Similarly, during fights to win mating rights with a female or to secure leadership of a wolfpack, the neck is often the target of preference during combat. In humans, tilting the head to expose the side of the neck is a signal of a willingness to adopt a vulnerable position. Whenever we want to display trust, commitment, approval, or interest, we bare our neck to others. It is almost as if we signal our surrender to the other person's will. In this way, we show that we are ready to listen, without contradiction. When someone listens to you with a tilted head, this is meant as an expression of confidence and an acceptance of what you are saying.

If you are involved in negotiations or are engaged in a debate and want to be interrupted less frequently by your opponent, try tilting your head slightly to the right. You can identify a negative attitude in your rival by one or more of the following nonverbal signs: hands in pockets, folded arms, a doubtful stroking of the chin, hands behind the back, tense shoulders, a dirty look, clasped hands, or the body turned away from you.

BARACK OBAMA AND HIS TILTED HEAD

President Barack Obama often held his head to one side when he took part in political debates. In animals, exposing the jugular vein in this way is a sign of trust. It is similar to the way a dog rolls on its back and displays it stomach, as a signal of surrender. In this manner, Obama showed understanding for his political opponents, who demonstrated less hostility and resistance as a result. Many of the photographs of Obama during his first presidential campaign depict him with his head in this tilted position, with the intention of emphasizing his interested expression as a means of uniting voters behind his cause.

Smiling

When you smile at someone, the recipient will often smile back, which creates a positive feeling between you. This happens more or less automatically. In prehistoric times, our ancestors used the smile to show that they had friendly intentions or belonged to the same group. Nowadays, smiles often serve to break the ice when we first meet someone

FRIENDLY INTENTIONS

new. Research has shown that if you smile and laugh regularly (so that it becomes second nature to you), your relations with other people will run more smoothly, last longer, and yield more positive results.

It is also a good idea to smile occasionally during conversations and discussions to show that you understand the other person. Some people have a habit of smiling too much, often to hide shyness. This reduces their self-confidence, which sometimes means that they are taken less seriously in a business context.

Eye Contact

In the West, we speak of eye contact as when someone looks her conversation partner in the eye at least 70 percent of the time. Fretz, Corn, Tuemmler, and Bellet proved in 1979 that good eye contact created a good bond between therapists and their patients. Seventy percent is a good guideline—any more can be seen as staring and come across as aggressive or just plain weird. In Asian cultures, eye contact occurs less frequently and for shorter durations than in the West. While in the West a reasonable amount of eye contact is generally viewed positively, in Asia it can be seen as disrespectful. Employees will often avoid making eye contact with their superiors, for example, not out of shyness or embarrassment, but out of respect.

Nodding Your Head

Giving a nod with your head is a signal of acceptance, a sign that you are listening. If you want someone to say something more, it is a good idea to nod your head and adopt an open body stance. This is one of the many gestures confirmed by Buli in 1983 as being conducive to creating a good and positive understanding in the course of a conversation.

**LISTENING,
PAYING
ATTENTION**

Mirroring Body Language

The mirroring of body language makes the other person feel accepted, which is a good first step toward mutual understanding. This mirroring occurs in a natural way between friends, loved ones, and people of the same status. Next time you have a warm and friendly conversation with someone, take a few seconds to look at his body language: You will quickly notice similarities with your own. In much the same manner, children frequently adopt the nonverbal movements of their parents. We are less keen to mirror people we don't know or like, such as the people we meet in an elevator or standing in a line.

Even so, mirroring body language is one of the most effective methods for immediately making good contact with others. If you meet someone important for the first time, try to copy their body position, movements, facial expressions, and the timbre of their voice. Make sure you don't mimic the other person too

APPROVAL, SIMILAR OPINIONS

closely, but perform a number of elements that are easy to simulate. After a short time, your conversation partner will subconsciously experience that they feel comfortable with you. People will remember you as someone who it is good to talk with. This happens because they see their own reflection mirrored in you.

Body Position

If you are listening to someone, it is best to lean slightly forward and nod gently. Focus your eyes on your conversation partner and tilt your head a little bit to the right. If you are talking to someone, make sure that your arms and legs are not crossed. If you are standing, keep your back upright: This allows you to breathe more deeply than with a bent back. A straight back lets people see that you are giving yourself the necessary room and air. As a result, they will be more prepared to listen to you, have more interest in what you say, and will take your opinions more seriously.

Relaxed Body Positions

When you are giving a presentation, the most important thing is to devote sufficient attention to the first few minutes. These are the moments when your audience gets their first impression of you. In this respect, body language is crucial. You can speak the same opening sentences in every presentation you do, but the way these sentences are interpreted by the participants will depend on your nonverbal communication. What you express with your body will also have a major impact on your voice and intonation.

This is the reason why many politicians take lessons from body language coaches: to improve the way they come across to the public. One of their most common mistakes is to try and reproduce movements and gestures that they have learned by rote, rather than trying to change the way they feel inside. When this happens, the movements and gestures always seem artificial: They do not give the impression of someone who is saying what they really feel.

For example, one of the reasons many voters in the 2016 U.S. presidential election felt that Hillary Clinton was inauthentic was because of her use of studied gestures and mannerisms. Rather than using natural gestures, she relied upon practiced movements which often appeared stiff and artificial. Her extensive training made her appear calm, but also somewhat insincere. Or consider the difference in body language between Barack Obama and Mitt Romney during the American presidential elections in 2012. It was clear that Obama was much more in touch with his emotions. This was evident from the synchronization between his gestures, his facial expressions, and his words. You had the feeling that what he was saying was authentic. With Romney, gestures and facial expressions were not always coordinated with his words. In fact, they were sometimes contradictory. This gave the impression that he had learned his lines well, but was not really convinced by his own arguments.

Our body language will betray us when we are uncertain or when we do not speak from the heart. The transformation of our body language must therefore always begin with the transformation of our inner feelings.

It is always a good idea to get yourself into the right mood for a presentation. You can do this, for example, by imagining that you are talking to friends. Observe in advance your own body language when you are relaxing with friends and try to transfer this to the podium. Do your best to ensure that you feel and behave in exactly the same way as when you are in comfortable and familiar surroundings.

Another good method (which works for some people) is to assume the qualities of a cat. Next time you look at a cat (or other animal), watch carefully the way it behaves. You will probably notice that a cat always seems relaxed, whether it is walking, sitting, or sleeping. Try to adopt this same relaxed, catlike attitude by sitting in a completely relaxed position. Think hard about this position until you find a posture where you feel wholly at ease. Do the same during a presentation: take up a stance where you feel comfortable, with your feet stable on the ground. If you feel comfortable with yourself, your audience will feel comfortable with you.

Pay Attention to Habits and Clothing

Clothes are another important element in making a good first impression. If you have your body language fully under control and use it correctly, you can probably come across as the "big boss" even if you are only wearing swimming trunks. In most situations, however, adjusting your clothing to the environment and the expectations of your conversation partner can help to positively influence the contact.

Clean and tidy clothes are a first signal of respect toward your listener. You have made an effort to look good for the occasion by putting on your best suit for her, and this is generally appreciated. Conversely, if you enter a room for a meeting dressed in baggy trousers and a moth-eaten sweater, the first impression you create will be a negative one. If you dress in a style that matches or reflects your conversation partner, that partner will experience the feeling that you already have something in common.

The same principles apply when you are preparing a presentation. Try to get a sense for the mentality of your audience. Think about how you can stimulate their interest and understanding. What will make them welcome you with a smile and warm applause?

A few years ago, we were giving a presentation in Qatar, where people dress in the traditional Arab manner. The men wore long white gowns with large sleeves and a headdress, while the women were wrapped from head to toe in black robes, with scarves that sometimes even covered their faces. The audience was there to learn more about body language. But what on earth could we do to try and build a rapport with them from the start?

First, we decided to wear clothing that was appropriate to the setting: long sleeves and legs fully covered. We also made sure that we didn't stand too close to each other and that we avoided hand gestures that might be considered offensive in that part of the world. Second, Patryk opened the presentation with a few simple sentences in Arabic, which immediately brought a round of applause. The ice was broken.

When you are visiting new and unknown locations, it is always useful to make inquiries about the local dress code and about correct ways to greet people. In Qatar, for example, it is the custom that men shake hands with men and women shake hands with women, but that men and women never shake hands with each other. It is valuable to know this in advance, so that you don't break any cultural taboos.

Another good example is a presentation that was given by one of our newly appointed trainers to a large group of recruitment consultants. The subject of the presentation, first impressions, seemed a good choice. Because we had seen him perform well a week earlier we didn't feel it was necessary to question him about his content in detail. To our—and the audience's—absolute amazement, he appeared on the podium dressed as a clown! He tried to convince this serious group of spectators to join him in singing a song, but the result was not as amusing as he anticipated and his audience turned against him. This underlines the need to think carefully about whether the things that interest and amuse you will also interest and amuse your audience.

THE IMPACT OF BOTOX ON BODY LANGUAGE

Researchers at the University of Southern California and Duke University have confirmed that the use of Botox reduces a person's capacity to empathize. The injection of Botox freezes the muscles of the face, which restricts the ability to mirror the facial expressions of others. By limiting the automatic operation of the mirror neurons, Botox users are less able to recreate the emotions they observe in others, which is an important way to make emotional connections with others and to display empathy. Columbia University reached much the same conclusions in their study of Botox.

What are the possible consequences? According to David Havas at the University of Wisconsin-Madison, "Botox selectively hinders the processing of our emotional language." Subsequent publications have translated this into an assumption that Botox can damage your friendships, because people can no longer read your empathy in your face.

Expressiveness

People like to listen to others with an attentive facial expression. Everyone prefers an open expression that encourages confidence to a closed poker face that encourages distrust. This was established in 1987 by Coker and Burgoon, and was confirmed a year later by the research of Friedman, Riggio, and Cassella.

Expressiveness of the face is just as important as expressiveness of the rest of the body. When the movement of the hands supports the words being spoken, it is easier to concentrate on what is actually being said. When someone is sitting, it is best to place the hands somewhere between the midriff and the chin, in the area of the so-called "Clinton box," which we will discuss in the next chapter. Of course, it is important that your expressiveness is in keeping with what you are hearing. For example, a strange or unexpected movement of the hands can appear aggressive or unreliable in certain circumstances.

SUMMARY	
Leaning the upper body forward	Positive attitude, interest
Opening the palms of the hand	Openness, honesty
Showing your wrists	Openness, sincerity
Hand movements near the mouth	Emphasizing words
Open hands on the table	Openness, acceptance
Talking with your hands	Illustrating words
The vertical handshake	Equality, good understanding
The handshake with both hands	Trust, warm feelings
Stretching out your legs	Interest, acceptance
Tilting your head to one side	Vulnerability, interest, understanding
Smiling	Friendly Intentions
Eye contact	Good, if practiced about 70 percent of the time
Nodding your head	Listening, paying attention
Mirroring body language	Approval, similar opinions

3

Positive
Body Language

Some years ago, we experienced a nasty surprise one morning, when we were giving a seminar to a group of well-known businessmen. That morning, Patryk had put on a nice shirt and an elegant pair of trousers, but when we arrived in the training room we discovered that he had forgotten to put on an equally smart pair of shoes. Instead, there he stood, in his Crocs sandals! As soon as the day's session started, I snuck out for a quarter of an hour to fetch Patryk's proper shoes from home, which he then put on during the first coffee break.

When the training resumed after the break, we asked the participants if they noticed any change in Patryk's appearance. The large majority said that they saw no difference. Or if they had seen something, they had already forgotten it—which sounds curious on the face of it, because the Crocs were really hard to miss!

So how did so many people miss them? The answer is simple: because Patryk gave the training with great self-confidence.

This chapter will tell you how you can also become so self-confident that no one will notice if you ever find yourself wearing the wrong shoes at the wrong time—even if they are Crocs. We will also look at the signals for self-confidence and dominance, and how you can recognize them. These movements, gestures, and expressions are often referred to as the *power positions*, because they reflect our internal power.

The Winner's Pose

SELF-CONFIDENCE

A self-confident person always adopts a winner's pose. This is characterized by the way you enter and dominate a space. The pose consists of a number of different elements which make clear to others that you are used to winning. You have the posture and the facial expression of a winner. Success comes naturally to you, so that you no longer even need to think about it. You are open, vibrant, and interested, with a relaxed but upright stance. It is as though your body seems to say: "I feel at home here; this is my territory." Winners enter a room in a comfortable manner, giving their body plenty of space. Their behavior is similar to a cat, which moves with fluidity and grace and always seems to be at ease in any position.

Relaxed Shoulders

SELF-CONFIDENCE, COURAGE

Self-confidence can also be displayed through relaxed shoulders and a visible neck. The shoulders are held slightly back, with the chest pushed slightly forward. This symbolizes enterprise, strength, and bravery. In prehistoric times, displaying your chest was already a signal of self-confidence, showing others that you had no fear of being wounded.

People who stand in an upright position usually look straight ahead of them and are not afraid to make eye contact. During a business meeting, people who push their chest out in this manner will find it easier to make themselves heard and will be listened to more carefully.

A Highly Mobile Jaw

Self-confidence is also characterized by a high level of mobility in the jaw when speaking. A wider opening of the lips during speech also helps to ensure better pronunciation. When we feel stressed or frightened, we have a tendency to contract the muscles of the jaw, so that we speak less clearly. There are exercises

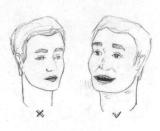

CONFIDENCE WHEN EXPRESSING YOURSELF

you can do to relax these jaw muscles. One of the simplest is to speak your own name while you are yawning. Of course, you need to do these exercises before your presentation or discussion—and not during!

An Upright Body Position

SELF-CONFIDENCE

People with a healthy self-esteem stretch their body out to its full height, so that they become two or three centimeters taller. They elongate their necks and look their conversation partners straight in the eye. If, for example, you watch a James Bond film, you will see that most of the heroes adopt this body position. In my experience, however, it is better to change one element of the Bond pose when you are conducting a business meeting: Try to make your smile warm and friendly, rather than cold and deadly. If your business partner experiences you as someone who is warm and friendly, she will also associate this feeling with the services you wish to offer her. The combination of friendliness and self-confidence increases your chances of success.

Relaxation as a Sign of Control

We mentioned in the previous chapter that a relaxed body is an important element in supporting good interactions with others. It is also a sign of self-confidence and control. If, for example, you work in recruiting and are conducting an interview with a candidate, a relaxed body posture is a good way to see just how self-confident this candidate really is. It is especially useful to pay attention to the moments during the interview when the candidate tenses and relaxes his body. The level of tension that the candidate displays when talking about his previous job can tell you much about his relationships with people at his former employer, how comfortable he felt there, and how much success he enjoyed. If his body is relaxed, this can be a sign that he received plenty of positive feedback.

The level of bodily tension and relaxation can also be used to assess how a person reacts to a particular question. If you ask a customer whether or not she has the necessary budget to make a purchase and if she suddenly becomes tense when she confirms that she does, this may be a sign that she is not telling the whole truth. Tension and relaxation of the muscles send out signals that show which elements of the conversation are more difficult for your conversation partners and which elements they feel more comfortable with.

Some people are used to working and conversing with permanently tensed muscles. In this way, the body shows that this person has very high expectations for herself. But will a tensed body actually help her to achieve her demanding objectives? Or will it hinder her? Who would you rather deal with in a customer service department, a tense person or a relaxed one?

We pick up the signals of tension in others at an unconscious level and have a tendency to avoid tense people, because they can seem to be a potential source of threats or problems. In contrast, a relaxed body gives the impression of someone who is in control, someone who will carry out his task in a reasoned and appropriate manner. If you have the habit of tensing your body at work, it may be a good idea to start yoga lessons, or go swimming more regularly, or to treat yourself to a relaxing massage. You will soon notice that closing deals with your customers becomes easier.

Looking Directly at People

Another sign of self-confidence is to look directly at your conversation partner, without excessive blinking and without breaking eye contact. If someone looks you straight in the eye when answering

SELF-CONFIDENCE

a question you have asked and if he accompanies this with congruent facial expressions but without actually touching his face, there is a good chance that he is not only speaking the truth but is also convinced by what he says. This was the main conclusion of Leathers's research in 1986. So, if you ask a customer whether she is enthusiastic about your new project and she answers convincingly that she is, without ever taking her eyes off you, you can interpret this as a sign that her enthusiasm and satisfaction are genuine.

Making a Pyramid with Your Hands

You can make a pyramid with your hands by pressing the tips of your lightly curved fingers against each other and tilting them forward at a slight angle. The hands can either be held high or low in this position; in other words, at chest level or stomach level. The high variant can often be seen in people who feel self-confident and superior, or in others who make limited use of body language but choose this hand

SELF-CONFIDENCE

movement to underline their own self-esteem. The same gesture is also frequently used in relationships between bosses and their subordinates.

Similarly, people in senior positions often display the hand pyramid when explaining tasks to others or giving advice. The same is true of people leading discussions, academics giving lectures, and politicians giving interviews. The gesture immediately suggests someone who knows what they are talking about and is master of the situation. For this reason, it is popular with experts in many different fields: directors, top salesmen, judges, tax specialists, etc. When people are self-confident, there is a strong likelihood that they will regularly make the pyramid to show that they are sure of themselves and convinced of the wisdom of what they say.

If a self-confident person is listening, the pyramid will usually be held at the lower stomach level. In both cases, the gesture is generally a positive sign, but it is important to note the body language that precedes the gesture. If the nonverbal language before the gesture was negative, the use of the pyramid can be seen as a confirmation of this negative opinion.

Holding the Ball

A variant of the pyramid is to hold your fingers in the same curved position, but instead of pressing the tips together you keep your hands some twenty to thirty centimeters apart. Because this is roughly the position the hands would take if holding a basketball, the gesture is now generally known as "holding the ball." Once again, it is a gesture that exudes self-confidence, but in a subtler and less threatening manner than the pyramid.

THE BALL OF STEVE JOBS

Steve Jobs's presentation style is world famous. One of the self-confident body positions he frequently used was to stand as though he was holding a ball, with his hands some twenty to thirty centimeters apart. In spite of his informal clothing, the use of holding the ball and other nonverbal signals typical of strong speakers made it possible for Jobs to project

SELF-CONFIDENCE

a powerful message to his audience. A good way to master your use of self-confident body language is to analyze video recordings of other compelling public speakers and regularly practice their poses and gestures in front of a mirror.

Thumbs Up

According to many scientists and traditions in various lands, the thumb is a symbol for the ego. When looking at the position and movement of the thumb(s), it is important to realize that a number of different interpretations are possible. Sometimes the thumb is a symbol of self-confidence, but it can also be used to signal control of a situation, hidden arrogance, or even controlled aggression. In some cultures, the raising of the thumb in an upward position—our familiar "okay" gesture—means that everything is fine or going well. Turning the thumb in a downward position means the opposite: that things are not fine or not going well. This gesture was inherited from the Romans and their gladiatorial contests. If the gladiator has fought well, the crowds gave him the thumbs up and he was spared. But if a beaten gladiator was given the thumbs down, it signaled his death.

OKAY,
EVERYTHING FINE

Pointing with Your Thumb

LACK OF RESPECT

Pointing with the thumb is generally used in contexts where you are laughing at someone or pointing at someone in a slightly disrespectful manner. The person making the gesture shows that she feels superior. Consequently, it is better not to use this hand movement when you are talking about your boss and your colleagues, since others will unconsciously interpret this as a sign of a lack of respect.

Thumbs Outside Your Pockets

We have already mentioned that the thumb symbolizes the ego. This means that standing with your hands in your pockets but

leaving your thumbs visible is another sign of self-confidence, but this time with an arrogant undertone. There are several variations of this pose. For example, if the hands are in the back pockets with the thumbs visible, the person in question is trying to hide dominant habits.

Women can use their thumbs to increase dominance. If a woman gesticu-

SELF-CONFIDENCE, ARROGANCE, OR SEXUAL INTEREST

lates with her thumb when speaking, this lends added weight to her words. You may notice that at the same time she is more inclined to stand on her toes, to make herself seem bigger.

Thumbs Behind Your Belt

If you put your thumbs behind your belt, so that your other fingers are placed on either side of your sexual organ, this can be an expression of aggression or sexual interest, depending on the context. In modern times, this was (and still is) a pose frequently used by cowboy heroes in Western movies, with the intention of showing the audience that the said hero was masculine. The pose is especially typical for the moment when the cowboy is ready to draw his gun, sure that his shot is going to hit home. The pose combines two different elements: the arms placed in a start position and the hands that emphasize the central part of the body.

Men adopt this position when they want to defend their territory or to demonstrate to rivals that they do not feel threatened. Women can also use the same position. This actually has its origins in the animal world. Apes have been observed with their fists on their hips and their thumbs pushed forward, in a gesture that suggests "I am the alpha male, I am the boss here!" It is one of the ways that male apes seek to attract a female mate. In a similar way, a man who turns his body toward a woman

SELF-CONFIDENCE, ARROGANCE, OR SEXUAL INTEREST

in this pose is giving a clear signal that he feels attracted to her and has sexual intentions.

Thumbs Up and Arms Crossed

If someone has her arms crossed with her thumbs raised in an upward position, this person is trying to distance herself from someone or something (crossed arms), while at the same time showing her dominance (thumbs pointing up). This is an interesting position, because the person in question might be trying to hide an arrogant opinion. You often see this position in conversations between subordinates and their bosses. The subordinate feels a need to show respect for the boss, but at the same time cannot hide that he has his own independent opinion, which he possibly thinks is better.

Hands on Hips

By placing both hands on your hips you show that you are ready to start something. A lighter version of this pose is to put just one hand on your hip. If, for example, you ask someone to take on a new project, this posture will show that she is ready to start. In much the same way, it is also a signal from a presenter that he is ready to start his presentation and that he feels confident about it. If you watch a presentation by two people, one of whom speaks while the other stands with her hands on her hips, this might mean that the second person agrees with what she is hearing and is ready to take further action or to add some supporting information.

Authoritative Hand Movements

Movements with the hands are among the nonverbal signals that exude the most authority and power. Sometimes it is not even necessary to speak to get your message across, because you can show exactly what you want other people to do using your hands alone. If you use your hands properly, they can give you a high degree of authority and the power to direct others. The following sections discuss the most common characteristics of self-confident body language signals given with the hands.

Pointing with the Index Finger

An index finger pointed in the direction of a conversation partner serves almost as a weapon for the speaker to increase the power and effectiveness of her arguments. This was probably also true in the seventeenth century, although back then people pointed swords or daggers at each other, rather than fingers. Today's nonverbal equivalent is often used during heated discussions. When the insides of the wrists are also shown, this might mean that the person concerned is trying to hide the weakness of his own position. Index fingers can also be pointed at activities that you are instructing someone to perform. For example, a parent might point to the untidy bedroom of one of her children, saying: "No iPad until you've cleared this mess up!"

In an American experiment, a speaker was asked to make a presentation to an audience with his palms up, which (as we know from the previous chapter) conveys openness and sincerity. Another group listened to a speaker with his palms turned down, which (as we read in this chapter) signals dominance. The third group had a speaker who was continually pointing his finger at them.

The results showed that in the third group one in every three members of the audience left the room before the presentation was over. Whether it was conscious or not, they felt the speaker was too aggressive (although they had trouble explaining why they thought so). Unconsciously experienced body language often prompts people to try and find more rational reasons to explain their negative opinions.

The index finger can also be used as a signal when we want to protect someone from something dangerous. For example, when we say "Don't go swimming in that lake, it's too risky" or "Don't eat at that Italian restaurant, my friend got food poisoning there." These messages can be

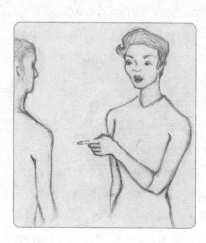

reinforced by pointing with the index finger. It shows the other person that we have important information we wish to impart, so that they would be wise to listen.

SETTING TASKS, DOMINANCE, AGGRESSION, OR WARNING

Hand Palms Turned Downward

DOMINANCE

As we learned in the previous chapter, open hand palms turned upward show that we have nothing to hide. It is a sign of honesty and openness. In this position, we can also stretch out our hand toward our conversation partner, to receive something from them. If, during a presentation, you ask a question and then stretch out an open hand with the palm upward toward a member of the audience, this person will immediately understand that you expect them to give an answer. If this person is next asked to take part in an exercise, they will probably agree. If, however, you ask the same things with your palm turned downward, this is a signal of dominance which may offend the other person and persuade them to withhold assistance.

The message is clear: If you want to ask someone something, do it with your palm turned upward. Otherwise, they might interpret your question as an order. A downward turned palm is used to indicate a task you expect someone to carry out; in other words, an instruction given by a superior person. The Hitler salute is an extreme example of this dominant hand gesture.

Sometimes, however, it can be useful to employ the palms down technique to display superiority and power. If you are standing in front of a class of noisy children, you can often get them to be quiet by raising your hands with lowered palms and saying "Silence please, boys and girls!" You can achieve the same effect by pointing your palms toward the ceiling or putting your hands in your pockets. Remember that using a dominant hand position when you don't need to emphasize your superiority can be counterproductive and can even cause hostility in others: Nobody likes to feel they are being ordered about.

THE PERSUASIVE POWER OF HUMAN TOUCH

In 1990, Major, Schmidlin, and Williams confirmed a number of hypotheses from previous research studies and gave added insights into the way men and women touch each other. Among other things, they asserted that:

- Women are more frequently touched than men.
- Men more frequently touch women than the other way around.
- Women touch other women more frequently than men touch other men.
- Women touch children more frequently than men.

Kleinke in 1977 and Willis and Hamm in 1980 conducted experiments which showed a correlation between the degree of touching and the power of persuasion. People who are touched when they are asked to do something (for example, sign a petition), are more likely to react positively than people who are not touched. Of course, it needs to be remembered that some people are intimidated by being touched. Even so, in broad terms it is clear that touching a person at the right moment in a tactful way and in a neutral place (for example, the upper arm) can increase your chance of persuading that person to do what you want.

The Authoritative Handshake

During a handshake, you can signal dominance by turning your hand in a downward position. It shouldn't be turned completely downward; just enough so that the top of your hand can be seen.

DOMINANCE, FEELING OF SUPERIORITY

This indicates to the other person that you want to take control.

When two dominant people meet each other, you sometimes notice them conducting a kind of fencing match with their hands, as each one tries to find the best angle to get his hand in the upper position during the handshake. This often happens, for example, when two politicians from opposing parties meet each other.

If someone offers you a dominant handshake, this is a clear sign that they want to dominate you. A confidently stretched out arm with the palm turned downward forces the other person into a subordinate position, so that he has to offer his own hand with the palm turned upward. This is a very aggressive way of greeting people and if you have little practical experience of body language it is difficult to avoid accepting the junior role.

One of the things you can do when offered a dominant hand-shake is to take a step forward immediately after your hands meet. This changes the position of the other person's hand and makes the handshake more equal. Another option is to place your left hand on top of the other person's right hand. Or you can use your left hand to give him a pat on the shoulder or to take hold of his upper arm. This, again, is often what politicians do when they meet a dominant opponent.

Hands Clasped Behind Your Back

Clasping your hands behind your back exudes confidence and power. It also automatically makes you take an upright posi-tion, since you can't bend your back if your hands are behind it. Thanks to the stretching effect this has on the body, the overall impression is imposing. The posture also exposes the sensitive re-gions of the stomach, heart, and neck.

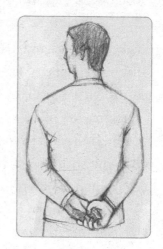

This signals that the person in question has the situation under control, so that they do not need to defend themselves. This is a body position you will often see policemen adopt when walking the beat. The same is true of managers su-pervising their staff. If you see someone walking around like this on a film set,

SELF-CONFIDENCE, HIGHER STATUS

they are probably the director. If you see someone doing the same thing at a conference, they are probably the organizer or one of the sponsors.

Hands Clasped Behind Your Head

When someone clasps their hands behind their head with their elbows stretched out on both sides, the person is very sure of himself. It is a position which says "I know better, I can solve the problem we have been discussing." In this way, he immediately tries to establish a psychological superiority over his conversation partner. People who adopt this pose like to tell others what to do, are happy to point out their colleagues' errors, and are not afraid to use sarcasm and irony.

ARROGANCE, "I KNOW BETTER"

A conversation with this type of person is never easy, because they expect you to recognize their superiority or complement their genius. At best, you can only hope to get them in a position where they more or less treat you as an equal. You can do this by trying to take the wind out of their sails; for example, by giving them a really complex problem or surprising them with information which shows that they are also capable of making mistakes. This will make them feel less self-assured, so that the position of their hands will gradually change. Perhaps they will stroke their chin—the gesture of someone thinking—when they start to tackle your complex problem. If it is appropriate in the context of your relationship, this is the moment when you should attempt to assert your own control of the situation by putting your own hands behind your head.

Of course, some people simply make a habit of putting their hands behind their head. As a rule, these tend to be arrogant-minded individuals. In most cases, their adoption of the pose is situation dependent. For example, when someone suddenly gets the feeling in the middle of a conversation that they are somehow better than the other person. Or when someone is close to providing a solution to a difficult problem that others can't see. It is also a gesture that can be used to signal that someone is about to make a decision. If this is preceded by a number of other positive body movements, the decision will probably also turn out to be positive.

Sitting Back to Front on a Chair

When a person sits with her chest against the back of a chair, this can either indicate an attempt to dominate, a desire to take control, or a wish to protect herself against attack. We feel more comfortable if we have a chair as a barrier between ourselves and our conversation partner, since this allows us to adopt a more open position. Having said that, this position can never be completely open, since the chair acts as

INCREASED SELF-CONFIDENCE THANKS TO PROTECTION OF THE BODY

a form of defense. It mimics the way people used to defend themselves with shields in medieval times. When we are protected by a shield or chair, we become bolder and more confident in the way we speak and the words we use. As a result, this position can sometimes be seen as confrontational.

When different people in a group start to attack one of the other group members, the target of the attack may turn his chair around and sit in this position, often just before he is ready to counterattack. The back-to-front posture gives him more confidence and allows him to place psychological distance between himself and the rest of the group.

Other objects can be used to create a similar barrier effect. For example, talking to someone through the window of a car door (instead of getting out) or the desk that separates the accountant from his customers and the director from her staff. This also explains why some women feel more comfortable when they have a handbag with them, which they can hold in front of their bodies as a form of protection.

Setting Your Feet Wide Apart

Standing with your feet set wide apart is a position mainly adopted by men. The position, which is often assumed without thinking, can make a strong impression on others. When a man stands like this, the person standing opposite him often imitates his action in order to protect his place in the group. The same posture can also be seen in young apes who seek to dominate their group. They prefer not to take the risk of being injured in a fight, and so instead of attacking each other the dominant males spread

DOMINANT POSITION

their feet as wide apart as they possibly can. The ape who can spread his feet the widest is accepted as the leader.

You can also adopt the same leg position when you are sitting. When I (Kasia) was a teenager, I regularly sat next to a man on my bus home who held his legs spread wide apart. One day, I suddenly realized that I unconsciously kept my knees tight together as a result. This made me angry: What right did he have to take more space than anyone else? After that, I tried to adopt the same legs spread posture whenever I could, to see if it had any impact on the person setting next to me. Normally, men adopt this position automatically when they sit down, without realizing that in this way they are hogging the room. I decided that the best remedy was to adopt the same position before anyone had the chance to come and sit next to me. I tested my idea out on the man in question and it worked: He was obliged to sit in a less dominant position.

Because this position is so typical of men, I found it fun to experiment in this way on my male fellow passengers. And it was interesting to see how it made them more inclined to accept me as one of them. They even began talking to me about different things.

Legs Crossed at a 90-Degree Angle

If someone crosses her legs in such a way that the top leg is held at a 90-degree angle, this shows that she's ready to discuss, debate, or argue. If, in addition, she then puts one hand on her ankle and the other on her knee or calf, this empha-sizes the strength of the gesture. It is a po-sition that exudes self-confidence, calm, and freedom from fear. Sometimes, how-ever, it can simply mean that the person in question feels comfortable with herself and those around her. The correct interpre-tation will usually depend on the context and the application of our five basic princi-ples of body language analysis.

READY TO ARGUE

THE SELF-CONFIDENCE OF BERLUSCONI

Italy's former Prime Minister Silvio Berlusconi frequently made the large, sweeping hand movements that characterize people with a self-confident and independent mindset. You can see this, for example, when he defended his country in front of the European Parliament. Or in the lecture he once gave to delegates from the Italian police, the Carabinieri, during which he made playful and expansive use of his mi-crophone. These are good examples of the way that large hand movements can make a powerful impression on others. Berlusconi was also an expert in making good use of his hands within the "Clinton box" (see p. 76).

Stretching Out Your Legs with Your Hands in Your Pockets

You can demonstrate self-confidence and control over the situation by stretching out your legs and putting your hands either in your pockets or on your hips. You often see this position adopted by senior managers, directors, and the owners of companies. If you want to know who has the final say in any given situation, this pose can help

READY TO ARGUE

you to identify who it is. The same position also signals a feeling of freedom when speaking or expressing an opinion. What's more, people are more inclined to listen carefully to what is being said.

Blowing Smoke Upward

In action films, you often see the leader of the gang or the mafia boss lean back in his chair when he is smoking a cigarette and very deliberately blow smoke in the direction of the ceiling. This

DOMINANCE OR FLIRTING IN WOMEN

is an action intended to underline his dominant position. A woman can also do the same thing if she wants to flirt with a man. In this case, she will usually first look him in the eyes and slightly lower her upper eyelids, which are both clear signals that she is interested.

The direction in which the smoke is blown—in this case, upward—shows that the person feels comfortable in the situation. Having a cigarette in hand can give some people an aura of added self-confidence. However, because smoking is now banned in so many public places, this gesture has lost some of its power. Nowadays, you can often see interesting scenes outside pubs and restaurants, where the smokers congregate. Smoking as a status symbol has been much weakened in recent years, largely as a result of the negative opinions held about smokers by the nonsmokers, who now form the majority. And it is certainly true that when you see a group of smokers huddled outside, often in freezing weather and without warm clothing, their body language no longer gives a dominant impression.

Large Hand Movements

CERTAINTY, INDEPENDENCE

CERTAINTY, INDEPENDENCE

Large hand movements, implemented calmly but decisively, emphasize a person's self-confidence. These are the hand movements used by leaders. They can be seen from afar and frequently have a compelling or intimidating effect. Such gestures are typical of people who are self-assured and not afraid to express opinions or take action. You see these gestures most commonly during speeches or business meetings, where they serve to inspire others to greater efforts. Most of the world's best speakers use this technique to get their message across more forcefully.

It is important to realize that we are not talking about broad, sweeping gestures. These influential hand movements must all take place within what has become known as the "Clinton box." The name is derived from American president, Bill Clinton, who in the early years of his political career had a habit of gesticulating wildly with his arms during speeches. This made a poor and uncertain impression on his listeners, giving the impression that he was untrustworthy. As a result, he sought advice from body language experts. Rather than preventing him from gesturing or teaching him new and unfamiliar mannerisms, his advisers persuaded him to restrict his arm and hand movements to the area bounded by his chest and stomach—and so the Clinton box was born.

By gesturing naturally but containing those gestures within a smaller space in front of his abdomen, Clinton was able to improve his communication style without coming across as fake. Except in a limited number of special circumstances, you signal greater self-confidence if you keep your hands firmly inside this box.

In the 2016 presidential election, it was interesting to see Hillary Clinton using the same body language technique in both speeches and debates.

POSITIVE BODY LANGUAGE AND ASSERTIVENESS SIGNALS

People who wish to appear assertive need to devote attention to the nonverbal signals they emit. Some positive nonverbal signals of assertiveness include:

- Congruence between verbal and nonverbal messages
- Relaxed body position and gestures, with the body slightly leaning forward
- Good eye contact without staring
- Decisive (but not expansive or threatening) hand movements
- A sufficiently loud voice
- An intonation that emphasizes the most important words
- Appropriate physical contact, with respect for others' personal space

Positive characteristics of a strong and confident body language include:

- An erect stance with a straight back
- A relaxed posture
- A calm but direct look
- Clear eye contact
- Dynamic and self-assured hand movements
- Good vocal rhythm and intonation
- Feet relatively wide apart
- Willing to initiate appropriate physical contact
- Nonverbal support of the interruption of the word flow
- Moving closer to the other person

Additional characteristics of self-confidence are:

- A relaxed neck, with the head pushed slightly forward and tilted slightly upward
- Ears positioned on the midline between the shoulders
- The torso relaxed and leaning slightly forward
- An erect back, stretched to its full extension
- Stretched legs with slightly bent knees
- Hips slightly tilted upward

The Boundary Between Self-confidence and Arrogance

The movements and postures described in this chapter are characteristic of self-confident people. But in many cases these same movements and postures can mean dominance or even arrogance and aggression. Body language always says more than words, and for this reason it is useful to ask where the boundary lies between self-confidence and arrogance.

A good position to analyze in this context is the pyramid hand position. On the one hand, this position is a sign of self-confidence; for example, if a candidate assumes the position during a job interview when speaking about previous employments or if an expert uses the pyramid while giving a fluent answer to an obviously difficult question. On the other hand, if you assume the pyramid pose too frequently during a daily contact situation, your conversation partner may interpret this as a sign that you want to appear superior. In this case, the gesture will act as a barrier rather than as a stimulus to smooth communication.

Nobody likes it if their conversation partner adopts a superior attitude. People have a need to feel that they are being treated as equals, that the value of their knowledge and opinions is recognized. Instead of promoting trust and underlining your knowledge, an exaggerated use of the pyramid can actually arouse resentment, especially in conversation partners who are also convinced of their own knowledge and expertise.

When both conversation partners are inclined to act superior, the conversation can evolve in one of two ways. If both parties give recognition to the other when they assume the pyramid position, the pyramid will support their communication, because they both feel that the balance in the relationship is equal. However, if they both persist in maintaining that they are right and the other person is wrong, the conversation can degenerate into a confrontation—which is what frequently happens in political debates. Sadly, this kind of "I-know-better-than-you" confrontation, where one person feels superior to the other, seldom leads to an agreement. Instead, it usually leads to an acrimonious and bitter dispute, in which both sides erect ever bigger barriers to communication, so that their opinions get further apart rather than closer together.

The pyramid can also be seen as arrogant if, for example, it is used too often by a speaker in a presentation or a trainer in a training session. This might give the audience the impression that the speaker does not properly recognize the audience's existing level of knowledge and is trying to come across as superior. Of course, it is acceptable for the speaker to use the pyramid if she is answering a question on a subject about which she is clearly knowledgeable, but even then, it is important to support this by using other communication-supportive gestures at the same time.

Most of the positions discussed in this chapter will give a positive impression of self-confidence if they are not used to excess. But if you do exaggerate, people will be more likely to think you are arrogant and superior. The hands-behind-the-head position is another case in point. At some moments in a conversation, this can be a signal that someone is sure of something: his opinion, the answer to a problem, the decision he is going to make, etc. However, if we see a person adopt this position with his legs stretched forward and spread wide, and if he otherwise demonstrates a superior attitude throughout the conversation, this will be interpreted as arrogance, so that people will no longer find it pleasant to talk with him.

A further example of two similar positions that can send out very different signals depending on the circumstances are having your hands on your hips or having your thumbs sticking out of your pockets. The hand-on-hip position shows self-confidence, but also implies openness and a willingness to take action. The thumbs-out-of-pockets pose suggests this same willingness to take action, but with the added implication that you are prepared for confrontation. In other words, the pose is both self-assured and aggressive. If a speaker were to adopt this position at the start of a presentation, she would find it very difficult to win over her audience. On the contrary, they would most probably turn against her, looking for weaknesses in her arguments and asking difficult questions.

Assertive Body Language

An important element of self-confidence is assertiveness. This is an attitude midway between shyness and aggression. Your message will have much greater impact if you speak in a calm but decisive voice, instead of shouting or acting in an irritated manner. Most people are inclined to ignore anything shouted at them—or to react aggressively. People who raise their voice are seldom listened to, which makes them even angrier.

We all have a built-in alarm mechanism which warns us about body language and voice intonations that are potentially threatening. If we detect signs of aggression in our conversation partner, our instinct is to counterattack rather than to try and understand what is being said. You almost need to be a Dalai Lama not to take offense or to react without irritation when someone screams and shouts at you.

If you express your opinions clearly, calmly, and firmly, there is a good chance that people will listen to you. What's more, they will listen carefully and respectfully. If your body language gives a relaxed and self-confident impression, it is likely that the situation will develop positively or will at least ensure that you are given a fair hearing.

SUMMARY	
The winner's pose	Self-confidence
Relaxed shoulders	Self-confidence, courage
A highly mobile jaw	Confidence when expressing yourself
An upright body position	Self-confidence
Looking directly at people	Self-confidence
Making a pyramid with your hand	Self-confidence
Holding the ball	Self-confidence
The thumb	Symbol for the ego
Thumbs up	Okay, everything fine
Pointing with your thumb	Lack of respect
Thumbs outside your pockets	Self-confidence, arrogance, or sexual interest
Thumbs behind your belt	Self-confidence, arrogance, or sexual interest
Thumbs up and arms crossed	Dominance, distancing yourself
Hands on hips	Ready for action
Pointing with the index finger	Setting tasks, dominance, aggression, or warning
Hand palms turned downward	Dominance
The dominant handshake	Dominance, feeling of superiority
Hands clasped behind your back	Self-confidence, higher status
Hands clasped behind your head	Arrogance, "I know better"

SUMMARY (cont.)	
Sitting back-to-front on a chair	Increased self-confidence thanks to the protection of the body
Setting your feet wide apart	Dominant position
Legs crossed at a 90-degree angle	Ready to argue
Stretching out your legs with your hands in your pockets	In control
Blowing smoke upward	Dominance or flirting with women
Large hand movements	Certainty, independence
Hand movements within the Clinton box	Trustworthiness, self-confidence

4

Negative Body Language

- How to avoid coming across as negative
- The best ways to react to someone's resistance and negative body language

In the sociology department of a university, I once met a professor who wrote fascinating and highly intelligent books. Surprisingly, his lectures were poorly attended despite their interesting subject matter. I decided to investigate. It quickly became apparent what the problem was: The professor seldom made eye contact with students, spent most of his time writing things on the board with his back to them, or else hid behind the tall lectern. If he asked a question, he never invited someone to answer with an outstretched arm but just launched his question into open space, in a manner that encouraged silence rather than response. As a result, he ended up answering most of his own questions. If one of the students did eventually say something, the professor crossed his arms, lowered his head, supported his chin with his hand, and stared intently at the student who was speaking. In short, the professor was a perfect example of a contact-breaking posture.

If you do not get the result you hope for during meetings or discussions at work, you may find yourself unconsciously slipping into this same contact-breaking posture. Look at the negative body positions in this chapter and think when you might have used them in the past. Also observe others and analyze which of these negative movements and gestures they display in their behavior.

Crossed Arms

**NEGATIVE OR
DEFENSIVE POSITION**

In certain circumstances, crossed arms can indicate a negative or protective attitude. You often see this in situations where someone does not feel comfortable or safe. For example, when people enter an open space full of people they don't know, or in an elevator or bus packed with strangers. In short, when others impinge on their private space and there is no room to put distance between themselves and these intruding others. In some countries, reading a book or a newspaper on a train can also be a way to isolate yourself from others, but crossed arms as a standard position to indicate you are feeling threatened or insecure is something you see all around the world.

Someone who uses both arms to protect his chest is building a barricade. He is trying to block something, which—in his eyes—is potentially dangerous and undesirable. Crossing your arms across your heart and lungs is an attempt to defend this vulnerable part of your body. It is an automatic response, and one that is also seen in chimpanzees and other species of primates.

If lots of people in an audience begin to cross their arms, this can be a signal that they don't fully understand what the speaker is saying or that they don't agree with what is being said. Many speakers are unable to reach their audience because they fail to see that most of them are sitting there with crossed arms. Of course, it is important to make a distinction between those who have their arms crossed all the time and those who cross their arms at a particular moment during the presentation. The more people who cross their arms at the same time, the stronger the signal. But don't forget our third basic principle for interpreting body language, and check to make sure that the cause of this collective gesture is not external (for example, because it has gotten colder in the room).

The tensed or cramped crossing of the arms can also indicate irritation or that someone needs to adopt a defensive position because she feels threatened. Crossed arms are clearly intended to serve as a barrier. Some people cross their arms to hide from an undesirable situation. By adopting this position, they show that a certain part of the conversation is threatening to them or relates to private matters that they do not wish to discuss. You will see a difference in their posture as soon as you change the subject.

Crossed Arms and Balled Fists

If the person you are talking to has already crossed his arms and then balls his fists, it means that his negative feelings are becoming more intense. When this happens, you need to be on the lookout for signs of nonverbal or even physical aggression. Clenched fists—often accompanied by pursed lips and lowered eyebrows—are always a sign of aggression and quite literally mean that the person is ready to attack. When this happens, you

need to change your strategy and attempt to calm your conversation partner. You can do this, for example, by asking a question ("Well, how would you solve the problem?") or by letting him say what he wants to say. If you ask a question, try to make it a question for which you can expect to receive a positive answer. Ask about solutions, not difficulties.

NEGATIVE AND AGGRESSIVE POSITION, READY FOR AN ATTACK

Arms Crossed and Gripping the Upper Arms

Sometimes people intensify the negative message of their crossed arms by gripping their upper arms. This signals growing tension; it is intended to emphasize isolation and a determination to resist any attempt to open up the arms, the body, and the conversation. The hands can sometimes grip the arms so hard that the fingers and knuckles turn white. At the same time, this form of hugging one-self gives the person concerned greater courage.

Crossing your arms can also be in-terpreted as a sign of stubbornness, as an unwillingness to do something. It is a nonverbal and firm form of denial, caused because the person in question is concerned about something or is op-posed to something. It is the kind of thing you see, for example, when well-intentioned friends attempt to persuade someone with fear of heights to go bungee jumping. Or when non-swimmers are en-couraged to jump in at the deep end. In a business context, this position can express that your conversation partner has no inten-tion of changing her mind. Whatever happens, she will refuse to accept this candidate or carry out that task, because it is against her better judgment. It shows that, come what may, she will con-tinue to dig in her heels. The only way to get her to change her opinion is through a long and calm conversation.

NEGATIVE, TENSE POSITION

Clasped Hands

In some situations, it is not possible or appropriate to cross your arms. When this happens, some people resort to secondary gestures and positions that carry the same meaning. One of these gestures is with the hands held low (or placed on a table) in a clasped position. This indicates a degree of nervousness,

NERVOUSNESS, UNCERTAINTY

insecurity, and a need for protection. As long ago as 1986, Ruback and Hopper contended that this gesture created a bad impression for job applicants, because it is similar to the gestures frequently used by liars. You sometimes see this in young conference organizers, who are better at organizing than presenting, when they nervously introduce their guest speakers. Children use this pose when they are ashamed or need to give a talk in class.

One Hand Grasping the Other

Another version of the partial barrier is one hand grasping another. This is a light form of the clasped hands gesture. Holding the hands in this way gives the person an added feeling of emotional security, similar to what she experienced as a child when her parents took hold of her hand at difficult or uncertain moments. It is a way to give yourself more courage and to create a barrier between yourself and others in a subtle manner. You can often see this position when someone feels awkward about standing in a group photo. Or when people need to give a talk or collect a prize in front of a large crowd.

Once again, however, interpretation is everything. If a number of people stand like this in a group photo, it does not mean that they are all feeling nervous and insecure, but rather that they are expressing group solidarity with each other by automatically copying each other's actions. When a person's level of unease and uncertainty is higher than normal, you will often see that he not only grasps one hand with another, but will also sometimes grasp his wrist or forearm.

PROTECTION, SHYNESS

Hidden Defensive Postures

In situations where very clear barriers made with the hands or arms are not appropriate—for example, in the case of public figures, who are aware of the negative impression created by such barriers—people still give expression to their need for protection and greater security in more subtle ways. They can do this by holding on to a sleeve, touching a piece of jewelry, or looking nervously at their watches. Women also do it by wearing a shawl or scarf, which they can then play with. In fact, women have more camouflage options in this respect than men, because they often carry a handbag, which can easily and unobtrusively be used as a shield and offers possibilities to "look for something" in a way that also serves as a defense mechanism. These movements and gestures are frequently adapted unconsciously, when levels of tension increase. But sometimes it is more deliberate.

Although we live in an age of mini-sized lapel-microphones, many speakers still prefer the traditional hand-held microphone or even a lectern-mounted microphone, because it puts something between them and the public that they can hide behind, which makes them feel safer. In the days when cufflinks were still popular, many men used to play with them in public, for example, when walking through a crowded dancehall. Nowadays, men have to conceal their nervousness by playing with their cellphones or holding a glass. You often see this at network meetings, where most of the participants have a glass of something in their hands to reduce the insecurity they feel at engaging a complete stranger in conversation.

Partial Arm Barrier

In some situations where it is not acceptable to fully cross your arms, because it gives the impression you are feeling overwhelmed, it is possible to adopt a less severe posture that only involves crossing one arm, with which you then grip the elbow of your other arm. When someone in this position is really irritated, you will often see them alternately stiffen and relax the stretched arm.

This partial arm barrier is frequently employed when people first meet each other, and feel nervous or insecure. The signal is subtle but clear. It is common in people who are constantly occupied in one way or another with people, but are overwhelmed by some of these encounters. The partial arm barrier gives them more control over their private space. For much the same reason, it can often be seen in celebrities, politicians, television presenters, and salesmen.

Another variant of the partial arm barrier is the bringing together of both hands in front of the body, but without one gripping the other. Interpretation of this movement can be confusing, because in many circumstances it does not have negative

connotations. However, when this position is suddenly assumed in a context that implies defensive behavior—for example, in combination with a step backward—it may express a need for greater protection. To reach an accurate conclusion, it is necessary to apply our five basic principles of interpretation.

MAINTAINING DISTANCE, INSECURITY

Gestures Accompanying Arm Barriers

Some movements and gestures can precede or simultaneously accompany full or partial arm barriers. This can include dropping your head between your shoulders, averting your gaze, or bowing your head or rubbing your hands together nervously. These movements and gestures all imply shyness, uncertainty, and a need for support.

Hiding Behind Furniture

When a child feels uncertain, because he is confronted with unknown children, adults, or animals, he will hide behind his parent's legs, hold on to them tightly, and watch to see how things develop from this position of safety. As we get older, we learn to control our body language better and make use of other barriers instead, such as our own legs (or hands or arms), objects, and pieces of furniture.

MAINTAINING DISTANCE, INSECURITY

In the previous chapter, we talked about how the body can be protected by the back of a chair or the door of a car. Assuming these positions allows us to feel safer and to speak with more confidence. In some cases, using fixed objects like chairs, tables, or other pieces of furniture as a form of barrier between you and others can help you to overcome nervousness and tension. It is easy to see the difference between the posture of a self-confident speaker, sitting firmly against the back of his chair, and an apprehensive speaker, who sits on the edge of the chair, gripping the armrests tightly.

You need to remember, however, that no matter what you are feeling inside, hiding behind furniture always serves as a barrier to effective communication. People like listening to others less in these circumstances. This leads to situations like the one we described at the beginning of the chapter, with the professor who was unable to attract the attention of his students because he isolated himself behind his lectern. Without this protective barrier, he would have been able to engage far better with the people he was supposed to be teaching.

Covering the Mouth

Some people hold a hand close to or in front of their mouths while they are speaking. Sometimes they add a little false cough, as a kind of justification for this movement. In extreme forms, people even push their lips together tightly. This is a protective gesture, designed to conceal doubt and a lack of self-confidence from others. Paradoxically, by doing this they actually create a negative impression. What's more, they require their conversation partner to work harder to listen, because in this position they speak less clearly and less distinctly. Of course, this makes it much more difficult for them to get their message across.

A sudden movement of the hand toward the lips is often a first signal that someone is about to stop speaking. It is possible that the person is momentarily confused or has had a stress-induced blackout, so that she no longer knows what to say. Covering the lips with the hand in this way can also mean that the person has said something she did not intend to say.

It is almost as if she wants to push the words back into her mouth or to punish her lips for letting the words slip out in the first place.

NOT WANTING TO SAY SOMETHING

Putting Your Fingers or Objects Into Your Mouth

Putting your fingers or some other object (a pen, the arm of your glasses, etc.) into your mouth hinders contact with others, because the objects represent a form of barrier, which diminishes the trust of your conversation partner. This has been confirmed on several occasions by independent research, including O'Hair, Cody, and McLaughlin in 1981, and O'Hair and Cody in 1983. Like covering the lips with your hand, putting something into your mouth that prevents your conversation partner from following the movement of your lips can cause irritation. This will also result in you talking more quietly and less clearly.

CONSOLING ONESELF

Dropping Your Head Between Your Shoulders

Another movement that weakens contact with others is attempting to hide or protect your head by dropping it down between your shoulders. This involves you tucking your chin into your neck and raising your shoulders on both sides. This movement usually accompanies an expectation of danger, such as a threatening subject that has just been introduced into the conversation or bad news that makes the recipient feel afraid and insecure. If the movement occurs suddenly, this may mean that the person wants to back off or shy away.

Regularly using the muscles that are associated with this movement can have an impact on long-term posture. You will see some people with a crooked back and others with a neck like a swan. The first type will usually be inclined to shrink into themselves when they receive news, whereas the second type will push their head forward, curious to hear more.

PROTECTING YOURSELF

Tapping with Your Fingers on the Table

Nespoulous and Lecours have characterized tapping with your fingers on the table as being "extra linguistic communication," a gesture that reflects an increasing degree of discomfort. In the context of a business conversation, someone who taps his fingers on the table is displaying nervousness. The more often and the faster he taps, the greater his degree of nervousness. If you notice someone displaying this behavior, it is advisable to try and change the focus of the conversation, until you discover the reason for his nervousness. If the tapping is a form of nonverbal comment on your proposal, you need to deal with this before the conversation can move on.

NERVOUSNESS

Turning Away Your Upper Body and Head

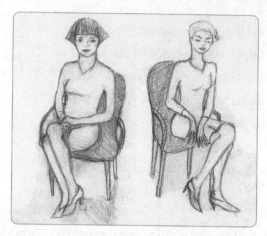

LACK OF INTEREST AND MAINTAINING DISTANCE

A lack of interest and a desire to keep your distance are displayed by turning away the front of your body. This message is enhanced if you also turn away your head. A person may turn away to hide her discomfort or because she is afraid of a confrontation with her conversation partner. It is inevitable that contact will be broken if you turn your face away from the person you are speaking with, because eye contact becomes impossible. Turning away your body (studied by Richmond, McCroskey, and Payne, 1987) has a negative effect on the level of sympathy you exude.

The front part of the upper body is the most important region for sending signals to others. If the navel and the shoulders are pointing in a different direction, that person's attention will unconsciously be focused elsewhere. Also look closely at the positioning of the feet and the direction in which they are pointing. Once again, you need to bear in mind the five basic principles when interpreting foot position, but in certain specific situations it can be a good indication of where the person is focusing her attention.

OPRAH'S RAPPORT TALK

During her decades-long career, Oprah Winfrey has interviewed many stars, and has discussed numerous difficult themes. What has made her so successful is the fact that she so seldom displays negative body language. During her interviews, she often shows her wrists and makes use of open and stimulating movements. This helps her conversation partners to relax and be more open, even in the presence of cameras and the artificial setting of a television studio.

Although many of her guests demonstrate resistance or negative body language, Oprah channels them back to openness by means of her own behavior. *Time* magazine described her innovative style of interviewing as "rapport talk," in contrast to the "report talk" that most presenters use. By dealing with the emotions of her conversation partners in an authentic and empathic way, she can nearly always transform negative body language into a win-win situation for both sides.

Holding Your Own Thumb

You may remember from the previous chapter that we described the thumbs as a sign of (among other things) self-confidence, which also represents the ego. When that ego loses confidence and needs protecting, people symbolically conceal

UNCERTAINTY, COMPLEXES, DEFENSIVENESS

their own thumb. Holding your thumb in the fingers of the same or other hand gives the impression that you are worried or uncertain, or that you suffer from complexes and have a defensive attitude.

Putting Your Hands in Your Pockets

Another body posture that breaks contact with others is putting your hands in your pockets. This pose can suggest a lack of commitment to the subject under discussion or can indicate that you want to distance yourself from your conversation partner. Alternatively, it might be reaction to what you see as approaching danger. Hands in pockets conceal uncertainty and allow the person in question to speak more fluently or even to attack with words. At the same time, the gesture can also have a compensatory meaning: it makes it possible to conceal inner insecurity

to such an extent that the person can permit himself to behave in an unfriendly or even arrogant manner. This is especially true when the hands in the pockets are balled into fists.

Keeping hands in pockets also demonstrates a lack of interest in taking action or taking part in an activity. The position can likewise be used to show that the person concerned feels no desire or need to show understanding for his conversation partners.

On a more positive note, hands in pockets can sometimes be a sign of relaxation and

LACK OF ENGAGEMENT, DEFENSIVENESS openness in a conversation between two people who have a positive attitude toward each other. But in official conversations, the gesture is more likely to be interpreted as one of indifference and therefore unfriendliness. When the hands are clenched and suddenly thrust into the pockets, this can signify a conscious breaking of contact with the other person, prior to launching a counterargument.

Giving a Stop Signal with Your Hand

When reporters want to put questions to a famous person as that person leaves a building or steps out of a car, the reporters will often be confronted by a raised and outstretched hand (or even two) in a *stop* gesture. This nonverbal reaction signals to the reporter that the celebrity does not want to talk and that it will be difficult to persuade her to the contrary. The gesture can often be accompanied by lowered eyes, so that eye contact with the reporter(s) is avoided.

PREVENT, PUT OFF, DELAY

Stopping someone by stretching your hand out in front of them expresses denial and rejection. You are sending a clear signal that you intend to protect yourself from something you do not want. If the fingers are spread or if you use two hands, this increases the strength of the signal, allowing you to maintain the distance you wish to put between you and others. In political speeches you can sometimes see a variant, when the palm of the hand is turned downward. (As mentioned in the previous chapter, this is a sign of dominance.) If a speaker wishes to encourage listeners to be quiet, this is the gesture she will use.

Hands on Knees

When someone suddenly leans forward and puts his hands on his thighs during a discussion, this signifies his disapproval of or lack of interest in the subject under discussion. It shows that the person is ready to bring the discussion to an end and to depart. In 1973, Knapp, Hart, and Friedrich included this position in their list of "inappropriate gestures" for ending a conversation. There is a variant in which the person places his hands on the side of his chair, as if to rise. Both variants are often accompanied by an angry look (with lowered eyebrows) or some other facial expression of disapproval.

DISAPPROVAL, WANTING TO LEAVE

Suddenly Stretching Your Legs

When a sitting person stretches out her legs to their full length in a quick and abrupt manner at an important moment during a discussion or when hearing something new, it means that she is not willing to change her own position and is preparing to parry and attack. If this is accompanied by crossed arms or by a backward movement of the head with stiffly held neck, it emphasizes the level of resistance to what has been said. They are ready to react actively against others or even move on to the attack themselves.

READY FOR CONFRONTATION

Hands on Hips

As mentioned in the previous chapter, placing your hands on your hips can be a signal that you are ready to take action. It is a self-confident gesture that indicates a desire to make progress. However, in other situations it can be interpreted as a signal of ag-

gression (especially if the hands are more clearly displayed and the body position is more imposing). It is a bit like when a peacock spreads its feathers, trying to intimidate rivals by making itself seem bigger than it is. If someone gives instructions with hands on hips, this underlines what

AGGRESSION, DOMINANCE

he sees as a dominant position. When someone receives instructions in this manner, it can cause irritation if the recipient does not regard himself as a subordinate. If a man uses the hands-on-hips pose in the presence of a woman, it means he is trying to impress her with his masculinity in a way that has a clear sexual undertone.

THE INDEX FINGER OF LYING POLITICIANS

It is an interesting phenomenon that people in the public eye who lie tend to use more aggressive gestures. They seem amazed when anybody dares to challenge or question them. Influenced by the emotion that always accompanies lying in front of a large audience, the simplest tactic is to try and mask nervousness with anger. The gesture that lying politicians frequently use is the pointing or wagging index finger. When being economical with the truth about accusations of fraud, President Nixon did this quite often and sometimes would even bang with his fist on his lectern. Bill Clinton also threateningly waved his index finger when he famously claimed "I did not have sexual relations with that woman."

Pointing with the Index Finger

We described in Chapter 3 how pointing with your index finger is a sign of dominance or of an intention to warn or chastise. It can also have a contact-breaking effect, because it unconsciously generates a negative reaction in your conversation partner. Waving your index finger around during a discussion will soon arouse hostility and animosity. When your position of authority does not give you the

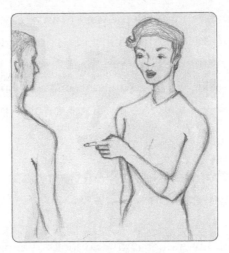

AGGRESSIVENESS

"right" to behave in this way, the people you are talking to may feel insulted and respond aggressively. Watch how many waved index fingers you can see in the heated cut-and-thrust of political debate. The same is true when couples argue.

If applied too often, the use of the index finger can also have a negative impact on children, since it creates a distance between parent and offspring; the child may feel unloved and unaccepted. The impact of this gesture can be strengthened by balling the remaining fingers of the hand into a fist. The tighter the fist, the more negative the gesture becomes. An additional level of negativity can be added by waving your finger rhythmically backward and forward in a threatening manner. This is the kind of gesture a headmaster might make when one of his pupils has done something seriously wrong. When this happens, the pupil will probably lower his head and feel pretty uncomfortable.

Because the index finger is unconsciously associated with so many negative connotations, we advise against using it to point at things on a board during your lecture or presentation. It is much better to indicate things with the wave of an open palm. This may require a bit of practice, since most of us are used to pointing at things with our fingers. However, the difference for your viewers is significant: They will find your presentation more enjoyable—and will pay more attention—if you use the open palm approach.

Lowering the Head and Putting on a Puzzled Expression

When a person lowers her chin and looks at someone in a way that allows this someone to see the white under the pupils of her eyes, this indicates negativity, criticism, or an aggressive attitude. A variation involves narrowing the eyes and furrowing the eyebrows. Both expressions promise trouble ahead if they are used in response to a proposal that you have just made. This means that your approach has not created the necessary degree of confidence in your conversation partner. Rather than carrying on in the same way, it is wiser to try a different tack. For example, you

can put forward different arguments or ask why the other person is so resistant to your ideas. Your aim should be to try and elicit more positive signals, such as an open stance, a forward-leaning body (usually a sign of interest), a genuine smile, or a contemplative, sideways look.

NEGATIVE ATTITUDE, CRITICISM

Moving the Head Back but Keeping the Neck Rigid

If someone moves his head backward but at the same time keeps his neck stiff, you should be prepared to expect counterarguments to what you have just said. Pulling your head back in this way indicates a wish to distance yourself from your conversation partner and his point of view. Holding the neck rigid underlines your strength of feeling. In this respect, the neck is an important part of the body for

DENIAL OR REJECTION

showing how flexible (or not) we are prepared to be. People with a stiff to tense neck tend generally to have stiff and inflexible ideas, so that they are less open to new ways of doing things and adjust less easily to the opinions of others.

Dropping the Head Between Raised and Tensed Shoulders

Pulling down your head between raised and tensed shoulders demonstrates a desire for protection, whatever the circumstances.

You can see this, for example, when someone in a moment of temporary insecurity cries out: "I really don't know what to do!" If the situation is not threatening, the shoulders will

PROTECTION, INSECURITY

soon relax again and return to their normal position. If, however, the person needs to think seriously about how to react, the shoulders will remain tensed, with the head tilted down. According to Harper (1985), people exhibiting this behavior are more likely to agree to accept a task or a proposal.

Raising the Head to the Horizontal

If someone is making us nervous or surprises us with a proposal to which we cannot agree, we often raise our heads quickly into a horizontal position, so that we can look directly at our conversation partner. This indicates that the conversation is entering a

confrontational phase and that our resistance has been triggered. Our head is like a control tower, and if we become aware that something is not right, we hold it at an angle so that we can see the source of the problem more clearly.

NOT IN AGREEMENT

Angling the Chin Upward

When you angle your chin upward, so that your head is slightly tilted back, displaying your neck rather than the jugular vein, this is a sign that you want to compare yourself with your conversation partner. It is a signal that says you feel superior. By exposing your vulnerable neck, you show that you have nothing to fear. As a result, this pose is often experienced by others as an expression of arrogant self-confidence. You will see this, for example, just before a street fight, with both sides wishing to establish their superiority before the punching and kicking starts. The pose is often accompanied by the elongated extension of the body, with the chest pushed forward and hands on hips. If someone reacts to you in this way during negotiations, this is not a good sign.

ARROGANCE, CONFRONTATION

Supporting the Head

When someone tilts her head to one side and supports it on her hand, this is generally a sign that she is feeling bored. And the more she tilts her head, the more bored she feels. Consequently,

this is a signal that implies criticism or a negative attitude toward what is being said. Variations on this theme include supporting your head with all your fingers on both cheeks or with your thumb under your chin.

BORED, NEGATIVE ATTITUDE

Crossing Your Legs

Crossed legs can have many different meanings, depending on the situation and the context. Consequently, it is important to apply our five basic principles of interpretation. For example, if a person

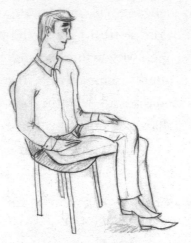

NEGATIVE ASSESSMENT

suddenly changes his position and crosses his legs, this is probably a nonverbal reaction to what he just heard, saw, or thought.
Similarly, if a person who usually sits with his legs alongside each
other suddenly crosses them at a crucial moment in a conversation, this can signify nervousness, resistance, or defensiveness.
This position has its origins in prehistoric times and is intended
to protect the genitals. However, it is important to remember that
crossing the legs can also signify other things. In certain circumstances, it can indicate shyness or modesty: for example, when
someone in a subordinate position feels he can learn something
from someone more senior or perhaps when watching a presentation or training course. Alternatively, it can simply be a useful
position when we want to put something on our knees, so that we
can take notes during a lecture or seminar.

In women, crossed legs do not, in general, have these negative associations, simply because they have been taught to adopt
this pose since childhood, especially when wearing a dress. As
a result, it has become a habit (even when wearing trousers),

rather than an expression of something. However, it can have significance if the crossing of the legs takes place at a specific moment in response to a particular situation.

Arms and Legs Crossed

When a person suddenly crosses both his arms and his legs, this indicates his wish to distance himself from the conversation partner and exit the discussion. All efforts to reestablish contact are likely to fail in the face of this double barrier. For some reason, this person either has no interest in what is being said or else has a completely different opinion, which he is not immediately prepared to reveal. If you are faced with this reaction, all

CREATING DISTANCE, NEGATIVE ATTITUDE

you can do is change the subject to something that is likely to elicit a more positive response. Asking a question that you know will get a favorable answer is one way to reduce resistance, so that you can then try to get your conversation back on track.

Legs Horizontal at 90 Degrees

When you put one leg over another at a 90-degree angle, this may (as we mentioned earlier) simply be an expression of self-confidence. However, in other contexts it might be a signal that you want to enter into discussion about something with which you do not agree. In this sense, it is a pose often seen immediately before arguments between men. Women are more likely to demonstrate their intention to argue in a different way.

The signal sent by this position is intensified if the person also takes hold of the horizontal leg. This is a sign that he will defend his own opinion stubbornly and will not easily be convinced to the contrary. In this way, the positive message of self-confidence is transformed into something negative.

READY FOR CONFRONTATION OR ARGUMENT

Crossed Ankles

If you suddenly cross your ankles at an important moment in a discussion, this indicates to your conversation partner that you have a negative or defensive attitude toward what is being said. It may also suggest that you are withholding information about this subject. If the position is accompanied by placing the hands on the knees or

DEFENSIVENESS, SOMETHING TO HIDE

by a nervous gripping of the wrist, it underlines the depth of the negative and critical feelings.

Closed Eyes

Closing your eyes generally means that you don't want to see something. If you have no interest in what is being said, but your conversation partner persists, you may perhaps close your eyes for a longer-than-normal period of time, so that you don't have to look at her. You can also see this if you watch someone examining newcomers as they enter a room. If the observer is interested in a new arrival, her eyes

CREATING DISTANCE,
LACK OF INTEREST

will open more widely; if uninterested, her eyes will fall shut.

Closing your eyes during a conversation can also be an attempt to break eye contact with the other person, when you have lost interest in the subject and are getting bored. This might even stimulate sleepiness during particularly tedious meetings.

If the closing of the eyes is accompanied by a backward tilting of the head, this can indicate a feeling of superiority. If you notice this in your conversation partner, you risk losing good contact with him, so that it is best to try a different conversational approach. Try not to confuse the closing of the eyes with an extended blink, which means something completely different—namely, a subtle nod of agreement or confirmation. You can notice the difference in the slower speed with which the eyes close (but don't forget to apply the five basic interpretive principles).

How Can You React to Negative Body Language?

There are many different movements, gestures, and poses that can break contact between people. The most obvious are the postures that set up barriers, such as crossing arms and legs, or adopting positions that create distance. These all indicate that the other person is not yet ready to talk with you openly. There can be numerous reasons for this, such as uncertainty, shyness, or a negative attitude (toward you or the subject under discussion). As a result, the other person is not convinced that they can trust you completely.

In these circumstances, it can help if you respond with more positive body language. However, you must also remember to check that you are not using body language that suggests too much self-confidence or even arrogance. It is quite possible that you are also creating barriers in this way, without being aware of it. If this is the case, correct your body language and relaunch the conversation.

A second type of negative body language involves the gestures that suggest aggressiveness. These include pointing with the index fingers, placing hands on hips, and raising the chin. Gestures of this kind inevitably lead to confrontation. If your conversation partner displays too many signs of aggression, ask him if you have said or done something to offend him. Sometimes a simple apology is enough to get your conversation back on track. Once again, it is possible that your own body language unconsciously projects superiority or arrogance, so that it is hardly surprising if the other person responds in the same negative way.

If none of the above is applicable to your conversation, you may be forced to conclude that the person opposite you is simply negative by nature. If you don't have to talk to her, then don't. But if you do have to talk to her, try to change the context of the conversation, perhaps by looking for a different location or changing the subject to one where you know you have more in common.

SUMMARY	
Crossed arms	Negative or defensive position
Crossed arms and balled fists	Negative and aggressive position, ready for an attack
Arms crossed and gripping the upper arms	Negative, tense position
Clasped hands	Nervousness, uncertainty
One hand grasping the other	Protection, shyness
Partial arm barrier	Maintaining distance, insecurity
Hiding behind furniture	Maintaining distance, insecurity
Covering the mouth	Not wanting to say something
Putting fingers or objects into your mouth	Consoling yourself
Dropping your head between your shoulders	Protecting yourself
Tapping your fingers on the table	Nervousness
Turning away your upper body and head	Lack of interest and maintaining distance
Holding your own thumb	Uncertainty, complexes, defensiveness
Putting your hands in your pockets	Lack of engagement, defensiveness
Giving a stop signal with your hand	Prevent, put off, delay

SUMMARY (cont.)	
Hands on knees	Disapproval, wanting to leave
Suddenly stretching your legs	Ready for confrontation
Hands on hips	Aggression, dominance
Pointing with the index finger	Aggressiveness
Lowered head, puzzled expression	Negative attitude, criticism
Head back, neck rigid	Denial, rejection
Dropped head, raised shoulders	Protection, insecurity
Raising the head to the horizontal	Not in agreement
Angling the chin upward	Arrogance, confrontation
Supporting the head	Bored, negative attitude
Crossing your legs	Negative assessment
Arms and legs crossed	Creating distance, negative attitude
Legs horizontal at 90 degrees	Ready for confrontation or argument
Crossed ankles	Defensiveness, something to hide
Closed eyes	Creating distance, lack of interest
Closed eyes, head tilted back	Creating distance, superiority

5

How Body Language
Reveals Emotions

- How the body reveals specific emotions
- What body language teaches us about relationships

During a discussion with an HR director about body language training for her management team, Patryk noticed that the director's body language was very open and positive. That could indicate (in fact, it did indicate) that she was positive about our proposals. She certainly had an open approach toward our project.

The situation changed completely when the CEO entered the room. It was as if the HR director was petrified. Her shoulders tensed, her voice became quieter, and she began to play with her hair. It was clear that she was afraid of her boss. The type of actions and gestures she used during the conversation with him gave clear information about the nature of their relationship. The relationship was based on subordination and dominance instead of trust, open partnership, and the free exchange of opinions.

The behavior of the CEO did not indicate a dominant personality, but he clearly wanted to create distance around his person. He did not allow others to read his thoughts. If you analyzed the situation closely, you could tell much more about the emotions and relationships of this man. Even a superficial analysis allowed us to learn much about the kind of emotions he engendered in his HR director, and therefore about the structure of the company.

> **" Body language reveals what a person really feels. "**

Nodding Yes

The confirmatory nod dates back to the Middle Ages. In many cultures, the short downward bow of the head is a sign of respect. In our daily conversations, it shows that we accept and agree with what the other person is saying.

There are, however, a number of exceptions. Like in Bulgaria, where nodding the head actually means no. And in Japan, where it means that someone is listening carefully, but not necessarily agreeing.

In Western countries, where we are more used to showing our feelings openly, the confirming nod of the head signals approval, especially when it is accompanied with a smile. If someone nods their head, it can also signify enthusiasm about what you are saying. As long ago as 1989, Remland and Jones emphasized that showing a positive reaction of this kind to the words of your conversation partner helps to support good communication.

ATTENTION, AGREEMENT, ACCEPTANCE, LISTENING

In business contexts, it can be useful to keep an eye out for the confirmatory nods of the person you are talking to. The first nod of the head generally gives a genuine answer, even if it is followed by a "no" shake just moments later. When this happens, it may mean that the person wants to hide his positive answer, perhaps as a negotiating tactic. As you have already learned, spontaneous body language never lies. A brief and unconscious "yes" nod can reveal someone's positive opinion in the middle of even the most heated discussions.

Shaking No

When a baby is no longer hungry, it shakes its head. Rotating the head from side to side on the neck is the easiest way to indicate *no* in situations of this kind, which is why this movement has acquired the meaning of refusal or denial in most cultures. The same movement can also be used when we experience the emotion of amazement, when something unexpected happens, or our conversation partner surprises us. However, when analyzing this gesture, it is crucial to remember our five basic interpretive principles. Because in other circumstances, shaking the head can have a very different meaning, or is simply a way to emphasize the emotions that a person is experiencing.

DISAGREEMENT, DENIAL, AMAZEMENT, EXPERIENCE OF EMOTIONS

Putting Objects or Fingers in Your Mouth

In the previous chapter, we discussed how putting things into your mouth can be a sign of insecurity. However, this gesture can also occur when someone is being put under pressure or puts herself under pressure. When we were young children, we were given a pacifier to put in our mouth, to make us stop crying. A pacifier symbolizes a feeling of safety.

UNCERTAINTY, IN NEED OF SAFETY

This explains why some adults still find it comforting to put something in their mouths at difficult moments. They do this unconsciously to feel safe. Putting your fingers in your mouth is an outward expression of an inner need for safety. But it doesn't have to be fingers: Cigarettes, pens, and the arm of your glasses can all serve the same function.

Playing with Your Hair

SHYNESS, UNEASE, SEDUCTION IN WOMEN

Touching your hair with your hand can be a sign of shyness or unease. This is not a modern habit, and can be observed in many old cultures. Today, you might see it, for example, when a manager is leading guests around her company for the first time, and is not sure how they are going to react. The same is true about someone who is introducing a new project at an important meeting. In a different context, women might play with their hair to attract the attention of or express their interest in a man, especially when it is accompanied by a seductive look.

Scratching Your Head

Scratching your head can be a sign of fear or uncertainty about something you want to say or do, particularly if you scratch with the right hand. (The right hand is connected to the rational left half of the brain.) By scratching your head with your right hand, you show that you don't know the answer to something and need help. If you make the same gesture with your left hand (connected to the emotional right half of your brain), this indicates that sooner or later you will probably find the answer on your own. In other words, lefthanded scratching signals temporary uncertainty rather than a need for help.

**WITH THE RIGHT HAND:
LACK OF KNOWLEDGE, IN NEED OF HELP**

Rubbing Your Chin

In certain situations, rubbing your chin can be a sign of insecurity—for example, when someone giving an answer is uncertain about the impression he is making on his listeners. You see the same gesture when someone who needs to give a decision is reflecting over the proposal that has just been made to him.

In these circumstances, be on the lookout for other signals that can indicate either a positive or negative response. Depending on the body language that accompanies the chin rubbing, you can probably deduce a nonverbal decision before your conversation partner opens his mouth to speak.

REFLECTION, INSECURITY

Covering Your Mouth

UNCERTAINTY, OVERWHELMED, FEAR

As we saw in the previous chapter, covering your mouth creates a barrier to communication. However, there are many ways you can put your hand in front of your mouth and they each send out a different message. In this section, we will look at the gesture where the flat of the palm of the hand is pressed against the lips, with the fingers relaxed and spread. This gesture may mean that the person is uncertain about something. It can also mean that a person has said something she instantly regrets or can be used to express disagreement with something that someone else has said. If someone is lying and experiences stress as a result, it could be that putting his hand in front of his mouth unconsciously puts him more at ease, because people will find it less easy to read the fear in his face.

Covering the mouth can also occur in other situations: for example, when you receive particularly bad or tragic news. This applies equally when we see an accident or something dangerous. The timing, the positioning, and the manner of placing the hand will allow you to distinguish between the gesture's different meanings.

BASIC EMOTIONS IN GESTURES

The most reliable information about what someone is feeling can be deduced from their microexpressions, the very short muscle contractions of the face that we will look at in more detail in Chapter 7. This special category of facial expression gives us information about the seven basic emotions, which mainly have their origin in our limbic system. You can often observe them before they are rationally made conscious. Traces of these seven emotions can be detected in the following body language signals.

- **Happiness:** gestures that express enthusiasm, such as rubbing the hands together or energetically nodding the head
- **Disgust:** avoiding gestures, such as putting your hand in front of you or turning your body away
- **Contempt:** gestures that express exaggerated self-confidence or arrogance, like putting your hands behind your head, lowering your chin, or tilting your head backward
- **Anger:** gestures of aggression, such as balled fists or hands behind the back
- **Fear:** gestures that betray uncertainty, such as hands shaking or dropping your head between your shoulders

- **Sadness:** gestures that create distance or show that a person wants to isolate themselves, such as stiffly held, defensive postures, the avoidance of eye contact, etc.
- **Surprise:** sudden movements that focus concentration, such as rapid blinking of the eyes or bending the body forward so that you can see better

Lowering the Eyes

When someone feels sad or stupid after they have said or done something inappropriate, they will spontaneously lower their eyes, as if they are looking at the floor. This expresses a feeling of uncertainty and unease, during which they no longer want to look their conversation partner in the eye. This breaking of eye

contact can also occur, for example, when a junior member of staff unexpectedly meets the big boss. By watching closely for this eye movement, you can learn a lot about the status of different people within a group.

UNCERTAINTY, SHYNESS

Slouching

If someone hunches their back at a given moment, this may signal a lack of motivation for further contact. This may reflect negative emotions toward the conversation partner, particularly if the slouching posture is accompanied by a severe look and a lowered (or raised) head. If you want to react forcefully to this kind of superior body language, you can counter the slouching by pushing your own chest forward.

LACK OF MOTIVATION

Shoulders Back

The opposite of slouching is pushing your shoulders back, so that your chest is pushed forward more visibly. This signals greater openness for contact and a willingness to listen with interest and attention. You often see this in the street, when a person meets someone they obviously like. Pushing your shoulders back displays enthusiasm and positive feelings.

OPENNESS, ATTENTION, INTEREST

Dropping Your Head Between Your Shoulders

FEAR, IN NEED OF PROTECTION

We looked at this in the previous chapter. Like a tortoise that withdraws its head into its shell when it is afraid, some people try to lower their heads between their raised shoulders. The tensed shoulders protect the neck, revealing emotions that generate a feeling of fear and a need for protection.

When someone tenses their shoulders in this way, it can also mean that they want to isolate themselves or distance themselves from the situation. This allows us to see that they are not interested in further conversation. Perhaps they feel overwhelmed and need some time to recover their composure. You can also see this same posture in some people with depression. On the other hand, it might just mean that a person is sad (or even just cold) because grief is a cold emotion, during which there is little energy circulating in the body. Fear is also a cold emotion, one that can give us goosebumps, in contrast to the warm emotion of anger, which makes us red in the face.

Letting Your Shoulders Sag

Letting your shoulders sag is a sign of surrender and weakness. You can see this, for
example, when a salesman has to report to
his boss that he has just lost a major customer
and knows there is nothing he can do to win
that customer back.

SURRENDER, WEAKNESS

Shrugging Your Shoulders

People use this gesture to indicate that they no longer have any
interest in continuing a conversation. It conveys indifference and
a lack of belief. You might see this, for example, when you try to
persuade someone to take on a difficult task. By shrugging his
shoulders, the other person shows that he thinks you are asking
something unreasonable and that he is not prepared to accept
your arguments and objections.

The same gesture can also signify a lack of willingness to
make a decision. Of course, it may just be that the person con-

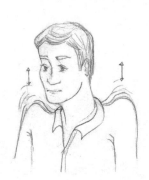

cerned simply does not know the answer.
In these circumstances, shrugging the
shoulders may be a gesture of irritation.
It is also used as a response to something
you don't want to hear.

**INDIFFERENCE, NOT KNOWING,
IRRITATION**

Clasping Your Hands

We earlier discussed clasping your hands as a sign of frustration. In some contexts, it can also be a way to hide your unease: for example, during an important interview or when you are worried about something. It can also conceal a negative attitude.

You can interpret this position in different ways, depending on the context and the situation. For example, someone might rest elbows on the table and hold her clasped hands in front of her face. Or the clasped hands might be laid on the table, or held under the stomach (when the person is standing). Whatever the position, the more white you can see in their knuckles, the greater the feelings of frustration.

FRUSTRATION, UNCERTAINTY

Rubbing Your Hands Together

A soccer player will rub her hands together when she sees a teammate about to take a penalty shot and expects a positive result. A car salesman will rub his hands together when a customer agrees to buy a new Mercedes. In these different contexts, the speed

FAST: GOOD FOR EVERYONE, SLOW: GOOD FOR YOURSELF

with which the hands are rubbed is significant. If someone rubs his hands together quickly, this is good for everyone; we will all be pleased with the result.

If, however, the car salesman only expects the result to have benefits for himself (for example, a serious commission on the sale that actually works to the disadvantage of the customer), he will probably rub his hands more slowly. This is the gesture you can often see used by the "baddies" in old films and cartoons, while they are dreaming up their next evil plan.

Gripping Your Wrist

FRUSTRATION, SELF-CONTROL

Gripping your wrist is a sign of frustration and an effort at self-control. The gesture can be made either in front of or behind the body. When it is made at the front, it also forms an arm barrier. When it is made behind the back, it is less noticeable and therefore less negative toward others. If the hand on the wrist you are gripping is balled, this usually signals suppressed irritation.

The wrist that is being gripped is also significant. Is it the left wrist, which is connected to the emotional right half of the brain, or is it the right wrist, connected to the rational left half of the brain? In addition, the higher the hand on the wrist and the more cramped the person's general posture, the greater their sense of frustration, especially if the arms are held behind the back.

Shaky Hands

If a person's hands are shaking, this is a clear sign that they are experiencing powerful emotions. This might be suppressed fear, which you can sometimes see in nervous speakers before they

begin a presentation, or controlled anger during a heated discussion or negotiation. Another variation of this gesture involves rapid and chaotic movements, although the meaning is broadly the same. Chaotic hand movements give the impression of in-congruence—a lack of agreement between the body and the words being spoken. As such, they are a sign of nervousness.

SUPPRESSED ANGER OR FEAR, NERVOUSNESS

Relaxed Wrists

The hands and the wrists play an important role in our nonverbal communication. It is therefore a good sign when your conversation partner has relaxed wrists, because this reflects openness and interest in what you have to say. When the partner speaks, it means positive intentions, attention for the other, and a reduced compulsion to convince. The origin of this positive association is to

OPENNESS, INTEREST, CONVINCING

be found in the fact that the wrists are also relaxed when stroking or when demonstrating physical sensitivity—providing the gesture is not counteracted by other more negative movements and gestures.

Stiff Hands

TENSION, STRESS

The opposite of relaxed wrists is stiff and jerky hand movements. This can indicate a lack of familiarity or good relations between conversation partners. It can also be a sign of tension and stress, when someone needs to keep a tight hold on emotions during a discussion. In 1975, Exline, Ellyson, and Long concluded that people who fail to show fluid body movements are perceived as being less competent. Stiff movement of the hands can be an additional signal to confirm controlled fear or anger. The rhythm of the movement will give more information about the possible interpretation.

Balled Fists

Since prehistoric times, balled fists have been a signal of hostile intentions. They indicate aggressiveness, anger, or controlled

ANGER, AGGRESSION

aggression. In business discussions, it is not possible (thankfully) to hit someone, but balled fists are a way of demonstrating the strength of emotion you feel.

Tapping Fingers

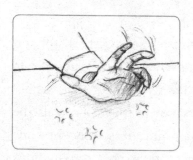

IRRITATION, IGNORING SOMEONE

In the previous chapter, we mentioned how playing with objects can make effective communication more difficult. Tapping with your fingers on a table or with your feet on the ground can be a similar expression of irritation, expressing disagreement with what is being said. It can also be a way of trying to ignore the other person, because what they say does not interest you. When this happens, it is advisable to try and identify the reason for the irritation or lack of interest before proceeding further with the conversation, by changing the subject or moving directly to the heart of the matter under discussion.

Feet Placed Firmly on the Ground

Placing your feet firmly on the ground is as important as solid roots for a tree. Firmly placed feet convey stability and self-confidence. You will not see this position in people who feel nervous or insecure. Relaxed and stable feet are a sign of balance and calm.

CERTAINTY, BALANCE

Legs or Feet Wide Apart

When the legs of a sitting person or the feet of a standing person occupy plenty of room, this means that the person feels calm and comfortable in his space. This is a sign of positive emotions, demonstrating willingness to show positivity to others. It also illustrates a high degree of self-confidence. It says, "I am not afraid, I am strong, I am important."

POSITIVE EMOTIONS, SELF-CONFIDENCE

Stiff Legs and Feet

As with stiff hands, stiff legs and feet give out negative signals. This might mean a lack of openness to the other person's story, a desire to keep a certain distance from the other, or even to withdraw from contact. Stiffness in the legs (and in the body in general) show that someone no longer has much interest in taking part in the conversation.

MAINTAINING DISTANCE, WITHDRAWAL

Showing Attention with Your Upper Body

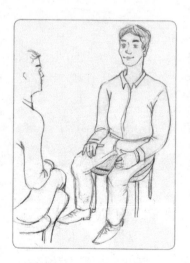

INTEREST, POSITIVE EMOTIONS

When someone points his stomach and upper body in your direction, without crossing his arms and legs, this is generally a good sign. It means he is paying attention and is interested in what you have to say. It is an expression of positive emotion, which can also be an indication of self-confidence.

Turning the Body Away, Changing Position

When someone sits opposite you with her body angled away, particularly if she regularly changes position, this is a way to try and avoid contact or confrontation. It is a signal that your conversation partner is not interested in the subject under discussion and has no desire to talk further. It is useful if you can notice when this happens in the course of a conversation, because it can help you to identify where things first went wrong. The same body posture can also signify unease or fear.

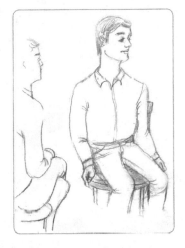

INTEREST, POSITIVE EMOTIONS

Sitting Stiffly on the Edge of Your Chair

Anyone who sits stiffly on the edge of their chair is clearly not doing this for their comfort. For some reason, they feel unable to sit in a more relaxed manner. Perhaps they feel insecure or are experiencing fear. It is certain that they feel in some way under pressure; otherwise, they would sit more comfortably.

INSECURITY, FEAR, TENSION

Not Moving Your Arms When Walking

UNEASE

When someone keeps his arms immobile at his side when walking, this expresses a sense of unease. This person is not comfortable in the space where he finds himself. Perhaps the location is unfamiliar or perhaps he is uncomfortable under the gaze of new people. You often see this behavior at parties or network meetings, where people feel ill at ease and walk around stiffly.

Relaxing Movements When Walking

STRESS, LETTING OFF STEAM

You sometimes see people who seem to move their head a lot when walking, suddenly tensing and relaxing their shoulders. This is a way to relieve the stress they obviously are feeling. You can often see this behavior in people who have just taken a break from the stress of the negotiating table.

SUMMARY	
Nodding yes	Attention, agreement, acceptance, listening
Shaking no	Disagreement, denial, amazement, experience of emotions
Objects or fingers in mouth	Uncertainty, in need of safety
Playing with your hair	Shyness, unease
Scratching your head	Right hand: lack of knowledge, in need Left hand: uncertainty
Rubbing your chin	Reflection, insecurity
Covering your mouth	Uncertainty, overwhelmed, fear
Lowering the eyes	Uncertainty, shyness
Slouching	Lack of motivation
Shoulders back	Openness, attention, interest
Dropping your head between your shoulders	Fear, in need of protection
Letting your shoulders sag	Surrender, weakness
Shrugging your shoulders	Indifference, not knowing, irritation
Clasping your hands	Frustration, uncertainty
Rubbing your hands together	Fast: good for everyone Slow: good for yourself
Gripping your wrist	Frustration, self-control
Shaky hands	Suppressed fear or anger, nervousness
Relaxed wrists	Openness, interest, convincing
Stiff hands	Tension, stress

SUMMARY (cont.)	
Balled fists	Anger, aggression
Tapping fingers	Irritation, ignoring someone
Feet placed firmly on the ground	Certainty, balance
Legs/feet wide apart	Positive emotions, self-confidence
Stiff legs and feet	Maintaining distance, withdrawal
Showing upper body attention	Interest, positive emotions
Turning the body away, changing position	Avoidance of contact or confrontation
Sitting on the edge of your chair	Insecurity, fear, tension
Immobile arms when walking	Unease
Relaxing movements when walking	Stress, letting off steam

6

Interpreting Facial Expressions

- How to interpret the most common facial expressions
- Information you can gather from someone's eyes
- How to tell a real smile from a false one

The face is our most important source of information about other people, because it is the part of the body that we see most easily, look at most frequently, and with which we communicate most readily.

In prehistoric times, the ability to read anger in someone else's face could mean the difference between life and death. Viewed from the perspective of evolution, it is interesting to note that the list of negative facial expressions is much longer than the list of positive ones. In this chapter, we will also discuss more expressions that have a negative connotation. This knowledge will help us to react appropriately to a negative scenario. Based on a quick glance at the face of our conversation partner, we should know what to do to try and restore good contact. If a person's facial expressions show pleasure, this is unnecessary since the lines of communication between you remain open.

A newborn baby can already distinguish between the shape of a human face and the shape of the other things around it. Research conducted on one-day-old babies revealed that they can identify the difference between various microexpressions, even though they are not yet able make these expressions themselves. The face is the most important external stimulus in our lives from the moment we are born. In this chapter, you will discover what information the face can give and what meanings this information can have. In the following chapter, we will examine a special category of facial expressions known as microexpressions, which reflect the seven basic emotions: anger, dislike, fear, surprise, pleasure, sorrow, and contempt.

Eye Contact

Eye contact plays a significant role in every conversation you have and is the basis for a good understanding between conversation partners. It is also via the eyes that first contact with others is made. It is important to realize that eye contact is often accompanied by other elements of body language, which also play an important part in your interaction, because they give additional or different meaning to the eye contact.

Staring

It is not a good idea to stare at someone for any length of time, because this will make them feel uncomfortable. When a person stands in front of you with tensed shoulders and an intense look in her eyes, this usually means only one thing: a desire for confrontation. A stubborn stare of this kind expresses threat. If we look critically at someone or something by fixing our gaze on a single point, this is often a precursor of a condemnation or a negative decision.

Staring takes away the privacy of the other. If a man stares at a woman from a distance, this means that he is attracted to her. However, the woman can find this uncomfortable if the attraction is not mutual. In this instance, staring will reduce the chances that the silent admirer will ever be able to start a conversation with the object of his affections.

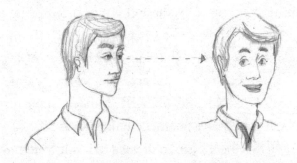

DESIRE FOR CONFRONTATION, SEXUAL INTEREST

When a woman is attracted to a man, she is more inclined to use a series of discreet looks, rather than a single long scare. If a woman is talking with two men and she is more attracted to one of them, she will look at him more frequently during the conversation. Loving couples often stare into each other's eyes, because they experience pleasure from being the subject of their partner's romantic gaze.

Avoiding Eye Contact

If someone seldom looks at their conversation partner, you might conclude that this person is not genuine or has something to hide. Avoiding eye contact means that the person does not feel comfortable in the wider contact process. If this happens, try to find out why. Of course, this behavior can have a

UNCERTAINTY, SHYNESS, SOMETHING TO HIDE

more significant meaning if it suddenly happens halfway through the conversation, when the person has previously had no problem in maintaining eye contact. In these circumstances, using our five basic interpretive principles from Chapter 1 is especially important.

The avoidance of eye contact can also be the result of shyness or insecurity. In some cultures—for example, in the Middle East— eye contact between men and women is avoided in business conversations, but is acceptable in other circumstances. If, as a woman, you are talking to a businessman dressed in a suit, you may be curious or even put off by this behavior, until he mentions that he has an Arab background. It is important to be curious about the origin or the reason for certain types of behavior before jumping to conclusions.

The Length of Eye Contact

In a business context in our Western culture, it is advisable to maintain eye contact with your conversation partner between

60 and 80 percent of the time, depending on the relevant power positions you both hold. If there are several participants in the conversation, the one who is looked at the most will be the most important. During negotiations, it is this person that most people will look to before speaking or making a proposal. This deliberate searching for eye contact is a request for nonverbal approval, almost like asking for permission to speak. If you watch out for this behavior, you can soon identify the person you most need to convince in order to bring your negotiations to a successful conclusion.

> **❝ Eye contact can show who you most need to convince. ❞**

If someone does not look at his conversation partner very often—for example, if he seems more interested in his computer or notes—this reduces the intensity of the contact and makes a poor impression on the person who feels ignored. Good timing and the right length of eye contact, appropriate to your conversation partner and your relationship, will help you to come across as reliable and trustworthy, so that both you and your intentions will be viewed positively. Looking someone straight in the eyes is generally regarded as a sign of genuineness and honesty. However, some good

EYE CONTACT FOR 60–80 PERCENT OF THE TIME CREATES CONFIDENCE

liars make use of this assumption and deliberately look into the eyes of their victims, to assess to what extent their lies are being believed. Fortunately, other incongruencies between their body language and their words often betray them—providing you know what to look for.

"" You need to keep a sharp eye on some liars. ""

The Pupils

Eckhard Hess, professor of psychology at the University of Chicago, pioneered research into the workings of the pupil and discovered that the size of the pupil changes if a person is more or less stimulated. In broad terms, our pupils get bigger when we look at something we associate with positive emotions. Hess noticed that in heterosexual men and women the pupils got bigger when they were shown naked photographs of the opposite sex. In another study, he concluded that the pupils of women are widest when they are shown images of babies, whereas with men photographs of attractive women have the biggest effect.

The pupils also increase in size when they are shown generally pleasant images, as opposed to unpleasant images of politicians, war, etc. Playing pleasant and unpleasant music also had the same effect. Last but not least, Hess concluded that the size of the pupil is closely related to the brain activity associated with the solving of problems. The pupils reach their maximum size when the problem is solved.

Larger Pupils

INTEREST, POSITIVE EMOTION, POSSIBLY FEAR

When you look at a person you like, your pupils will probably become larger. The same is true when you are offered something advantageous. Our pupils react by increasing in size in response to positive emotional experiences, such as interest, love, and sympathy. Intensive thought can also have the same effect. Because larger pupils are associated with positive experiences, people with such pupils often seem more attractive and more sympathetic. It is for this reason that the pupils of women in advertising photographs for perfume or cosmetics are nowadays digitally reworked. However, there is one exception to the above of which you need to be aware: Great fear can also result in very large pupils. In general, pupils can increase or decrease in size by 400 percent.

Smaller Pupils

LACK OF INTEREST, NEGATIVE EMOTIONS

The pupils get smaller when our interest is not genuine. Our pupils reduce in size when we are faced with an admirer who we do not really like. Of course, it is only possible to make such assessments when the amount and fall of light remains the same (pupils react automatically to changing light). Similarly, you need to have a good idea of the person's normal pupil size before you can make a valid comparison.

PUPILS IN PRACTICE

Following Hess's research into the changing size of pupils, a number of other studies were conducted, most of which reached broadly the same conclusions. We have conducted our own tests into this subject, using photographs that call up different emotions and filming the reaction of people's faces with a powerful zoom lens. Our results concurred with the majority of the previous studies—namely, that the pupils change in size by about 10 percent in response to relatively strong positive or negative stimuli. However, this quantification of 10 percent is a crucial element that was lacking in many of the existing research results. It is crucial because a change of 10 percent equates to a change of less than half a millimeter. In other words, at normal conversational distance, it is impossible to observe the change in pupil size with the naked eye, even in the presence of powerful stimuli. Consequently, in the context of business negotiations you are likely to learn more about your conversation partner from her other body language than by trying to stare deeply into her eyes to see what her pupils are doing.

Eyes and Eyelids

The eyes and eyelids play a leading role in the communication process. Eye movements offer plenty of information for useful analysis. For example, in the traditional dance of Kerala in southern India the performers tell the story using just eye and hand movements. Similarly, the eyes are an important part of Arabian, Persian, and Turkish culture. Here are some interpretations that might help you in your own context.

Larger Eyes

By raising your upper eyelid more than normal, you can communicate amazement or surprise. If the movement is more exaggerated and held for longer, it can express fear. In both cases, it is often associated with a similar raising of the eyebrows. For surprise, the eyebrows are tensed, while for fear the tension is more obviously in the forehead.

AMAZEMENT

Quick Exchange of Looks

EXCHANGE OF INFORMATION

A quick exchange of looks between two people, often performed simultaneously and unnoticed by others, can involve a secret exchange of information or opinions about the subject under discussion.

Angry Look

An angry look that is clearly targeted at someone, with the eyes narrowed and the eyebrows turned down, is an expression of dis-

pleasure, superiority, or contempt. The context of this look is important, because it can also occur when a person is concentrating hard or cannot see something properly. In neither of these cases is the person necessarily angry.

DISPLEASURE, SUPERIORITY, CONTEMPT

Winking

If someone gives you a wink and keeps on looking at you, this is usually intended as a way to attract your attention. Gener-

ally, the person wishes to confirm something positive or warn you of something negative.

ATTRACTING ATTENTION, WARNING

Confirmatory Blinking

CONFIRMATION, AGREEMENT

Briefly closing your eyes and then quickly opening them again can indicate confirmation or approval to the person you are looking at. It is a variant of nodding your head.

Sideways Glance

A sideways glance with your eyes, with your head also slightly turned sideways, can be used to signal disbelief, reluctance, distrust, or disapproval. Confusingly, it can also signify interest, depending on the other body language that accompanies the

glance. When the eyebrows are slightly raised during the sideways glance, or if it is accompanied by a slight smile, it is a sign of interest. If the eyebrows and the corners of the mouth are turned down, it is hostile and negative in intent.

DISBELIEF, RELUCTANCE, DISTRUST, OR DISAPPROVAL

Narrowing the Eyes

Narrowing the eyes can mean several things. It can be a request for more information—not for knowledge in general, but for more details about a subject already known. It can also be a sign of deep concentration on one specific thing, when we narrow the focus of our attention like the zoom lens on a camera. If your conversation partner narrows her eyes, you can expect one of two possibilities: It can either be a precursor to asking a specific question about something she has not understood, or else it can signify that she is thinking hard about something that has just been said or she is about to say. In this latter instance, you do not need to react. When the person relaxes her eyes again, she has finished her thinking and is ready to continue the conversation.

REQUEST FOR MORE INFORMATION, CONCENTRATION, ANGER

Do not let yourself be misled by people who assume this expression frequently during negotiations or interviews. It may mean that they want more details about your proposal so that they can critically assess it, but it can also just be something they do from habit in this kind of discussion. This may give the impression that they are severe, when this is not really what they intend. This same eye movement can also be a microexpression of anger when it lasts for less than half a second. So how do you know which of these interpretations is the right one? By using our five basic principles.

Blinking Your Eyes

Blinking serves the important function of keeping the eyes sufficiently moist and clean. When we are relaxed, we blink between six and eight times each minute, closing our eyelids each time for about a tenth of a second.

Research by the neuro-scientist Daniel Smilek, at the University of Waterloo, has shown that people who display less attention or whose thoughts are elsewhere blink more. In this way, they are able to isolate themselves more from what is happening around them.

The traditional assertion that liars blink more is simply not true. Dr. Sharon Leal of Portsmouth University has proven that liars

actually blink less when they are lying, because the brain is working more intensely to fabricate the lie. As a consequence, after the lie has been told and their level of tension has

FAST BLINKING NECESSARY AFTER INTENSIVE THINKING

been lowered, they need to compensate for this reduced blinking by blinking more than one would normally expect.

" It is a myth that liars blink more when they are lying. "

Averting Your Gaze

When you are talking about something neutral or pleasant and the face of your conversation partner betrays that something is wrong (for example, if his facial muscles suddenly tense), he may well suddenly look away, in order to break eye contact so that he can more clearly focus on his own inner thoughts. Perhaps this person has something to hide that the conversation has unexpectedly brought to mind, so that he needs a brief period to restructure his thoughts. To accomplish this, he temporarily breaks off the communication by averting his gaze. It is important to

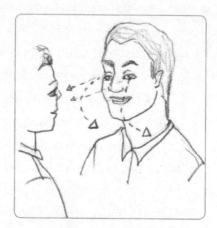

HIDING SOMETHING, NEEDING DISTANCE

note how long this interruption lasts. If he reestablishes eye contact after only a brief pause, this means that he is once again concentrating on what you are saying. If the interruption lasts for a longer period, there is a risk that your communication will become purely one dimensional, because the person for whom it is intended is no longer listening.

Burgoon, Manusov, Mineo, and Hale warn that people who avert their gaze before answering a question and who in general maintain less eye contact during conversations are more likely to be regarded as less competent. In such situations, your conversation partner has almost literally run away with his eyes.

We tend to avert our gaze when we want to avoid giving an opinion or escape from doing something that does not appeal to us. The necessary information is still communicated in our direction, so we try to ignore it by looking away. In this way, we hope to sidestep the confrontation. When faced with situations of this kind, it is important to note what other body language is being displayed. Only then will you know how best to react.

EXPLAINING THE MYTHS AROUND EYE MOVEMENT

You have probably heard that you can tell whether someone is lying by watching closely the direction of their eye movements. This myth is often associated with NLP (Neuro-Linguistic Programming), developed by Grinder and Bandler. However, the so-called developers of NLP never included it in their original research findings and there have been an insufficient number of other studies to prove that you can detect when someone is lying simply by following their eye movements. Conversely, it has not been possible to prove the opposite hypothesis. The eye-movement theory was originally only referred to as an NLP model. The myth that you can detect liars by following their eyes was spread primarily by the nonscientific media. Although this misinterpretation of the original research findings has spread like wildfire, the truth is that there is insufficient evidence to prove or disprove the theory.

Raising Your Eyebrows

Before we discuss the different possible interpretations for raised eyebrows, it is important to again emphasize the importance of applying our five basic principles when trying to assess what this facial movement really means. Depending on the context and the timing, it can be a sign of surprise, when someone hears something unusual or even incredible. If the expression lasts for longer, this may be deliberate, because the person wishes to express amazement rather than just surprise. In a different context, raised eyebrows can signal admiration—for example, when your colleague has just bought a brand-new sports car.

It is a complicating factor that many people use their eyebrows to emphasize words in general conversation. This means that you need to first calibrate this normal use of the eyebrows in a

number of ordinary and unimportant situations, so that you can correctly assess when the use becomes exceptional in other circumstances, when perhaps there is more at stake.

SURPRISE, GREETING

The short raising of the eyebrows when still at a distance from the other person has been used since prehistoric times as a greeting or a sign that you have noticed their approach. It serves to momentarily attract the attention of the other party. It can also be useful in male-female relations, when it can sometimes have a sexual undertone. If you raise your eyebrows toward a person you do not know, this might make them think that you are not, in fact, unknown to them, which will put them more at ease. It is also an expression that you can use in much the same way at network meetings, to help you make contact with new people, particularly if it is accompanied by a smile. In the 1970s, Professor Mark Knapp concluded that this gesture was a good way to get a conversation started.

Raising One Eyebrow

DISBELIEF

Raising a single eyebrow (it doesn't matter which one) is an expression of disbelief. The eyebrow that isn't raised is often lowered slightly. This makes this facial movement a combination of both surprise (eyebrows raised) and a negative assessment (eyebrows lowered). Because it is impossible to raise and lower both your eyebrows simultaneously, when people encounter a surprise that they view with disbelief, one eyebrow is raised while the other is lowered or remains tensed in position.

If someone transmits this signal while you are explaining something, it is probably wise either to adjust your line of argument, or give additional clarification in support of those arguments, or simply ask the other person why they look so surprised. If you fail to do this, there is a possibility that the negative assessment of your conversation partner will boomerang against you later in the discussion or negotiation. As always, however, remember to apply the five basic principles of interpretation when formulating your conclusions. It may be that your conversation partner regularly makes this expression for no particular reason. The person using this expression gives the impression of being strong and critical, whereas that might not be the case.

Ignoring a raised eyebrow can come back to hit you like a boomerang.

Lowering Your Eyebrows

Lowering both eyebrows, so that vertical lines appear above your nose, can be an expression of dissatisfaction, anger, or an unpleasant surprise. If the movement is short, it may just signify the experiencing of emotions. If it is held for any length of time, this is more likely an attempt to signify displeasure. Some people use this expression deliberately, to appear stricter than they actually are. However, research by Forbes and Jackson in 1980 showed that job candidates who lowered their eyebrows were less likely to be selected than candidates who smiled,

DISSATISFACTION, ANGER, OR
UNPLEASANT SURPRISE

irrespective of their competencies and other factors. So be careful if you are someone who frequently pulls down your eyebrows for no reason. You could be giving the wrong impression!

Pursed Lips

If the lips are pressed together for a half second or shorter, in some circumstances this can be a microexpression of controlled anger or sorrow. However, pursed lips can also convey other signals, such as a lack of acceptance. This disapproval can be a reaction to a proposal or to the behavior of someone who does not match up to the expectations of the person doing the pursing. It is an expression which shows the other person that they should be ready for resistance or criticism.

Alternatively, pursed lips can also mean that the person concerned does not intend to share information they know. In this case, the expression underlines their determination not to speak, so you know that it will not be easy to get this information out

of them verbally. Fortunately, a good understanding of their other body language will help you to learn what you need to know in other ways. This is the essence of our BLINK Conversation Technique™, which we will discuss in Chapter 8.

**LACK OF ACCEPTANCE,
NOT WANTING TO SAY SOMETHING**

A Real or False Smile

A real, genuine smile involves the simultaneous contraction of two groups of muscles: the muscles around the eye (orbicularis oculi) and the muscles above the mouth (zygomatic major). We learn to recognize these signals when we are babies. When babies see their smiling mother, they make a connection between the smile and a pleasing solution to the problem of feeling hungry. Because of the positive connotations associated with this signal, it is generally used as an element in the ceremony of meeting someone new.

The type of smile a person uses can give you a glimpse at what they are feeling when they meet you. If, for example, the smile is not real, so that the teeth are exposed between taut lips, this person is probably trying to project superiority: "Look at me! I've got teeth! I can bite!" The arsenal of different smiles is immense, ranging from smiles that signal disapproval to happiness to enmity to pleasant surprise.

The difference between genuine and false happiness can be easily identified by looking at the eyes. In his 1862 book, the psychologist Duchenne recorded that the experiencing of real

Top left: REAL SMILE: CONTRACTION OF THE ORBICULARIS OCULI (EYE CORNERS STRETCHED, EYEBROWS LOWERED)

Top right: FALSE SMILE: ONLY WITH THE MOUTH

happiness is accompanied by the contraction of the orbicularis oculi muscle. This means that the piece of skin between the eye and the outer edge of the eyebrow is stretched and pulled slightly downward, while the eyebrow itself is often slightly lowered. As a result, you will usually see more wrinkles around the eye when this happens (unless the person you are looking at has used Botox). However, the fact that you see wrinkles around the eyes is not, by itself, sufficient to conclude that the smile is genuine. Some people already have these wrinkles and the simple contraction of the zygomatic major muscle can make them appear, without the need to contract the orbicularis oculi muscle.

Since 1862, numerous studies have confirmed the hypothesis of the genuine Duchenne smile, as well as establishing that the contraction of the orbicularis oculi muscle occurs in conjunction with higher alpha-activity in the left pre-frontal cortex. However, since 2009 a number of research projects have cast doubt on this generally accepted wisdom. For example, one study showed that 70 percent of people are capable of faking a Duchenne smile when they are shown a photograph of a genuine smile. Unfortunately, a study to analyze the faking of a smile in negative situations has not yet been conducted.

Until more conclusive research has been carried out, we remain of the opinion that you can often recognize a fraudulent smile by the way the eyes are contracted. If the orbicularis oculi muscle is consciously and deliberately contracted, without the person experiencing genuine pleasure, you should be able to notice that the smile seems tenser, as if it is posed. You will probably also see that the orbicularis oculi pars orbitalis muscles contract, but that the orbicularis oculi pars palpebralis muscles (the muscles around the underside of the eye) are more relaxed.

Other elements can also help you to spot the difference. Research has shown that a false smile is more exaggerated on one side of the face. With a genuine smile, both halves of the brain send out the same signal. With a fake smile, the part of the brain that is specialized in facial expressions—located in the right half—sends more conscious signals to the left side of the body. This means that fake emotions are more likely to display themselves on this left side. When emotions are experienced spontaneously and unconsciously, both halves of the brain work symmetrically.

Once again you need to apply the five basic interpretive principles and you also need a reliable basis for comparison between how a person looks when they are smiling genuinely or just pretending. Some people normally smile asymmetrically.

THE IMPACT OF ALCOHOL ON YOUR LAUGHING MUSCLES

Between 1990 and 1996, Willibard Ruch carried out a number of fascinating studies into humor and emotions, as well as the effects of alcohol on body language. You might expect that people under the influence of alcohol would laugh more. This hypothesis is broadly correct, if the quantity of alcohol remains limited. However, his research also showed that even extroverted people under the influence of a significant amount of alcohol display fewer expressions of pleasure in their face.

Research into Eyes and Their Power of Persuasion

The eyes play an important role in interpersonal relations, because they indicate a willingness to communicate. In 1976, Argyle and Cook emphasized that looking at someone always conveys a meaning, because it shows that the two people concerned are engaged with each other. The eyes and their movements not only signal that both people have noticed each other, but also reflect degrees of mutual interest.

According to Harper, Wiens, and Matarazzo, the eyes also have an important function relating to changes in the distribution of relative power within relationships. A person who wishes to be convincing or appear reliable needs to maintain eye contact both when she is speaking and listening. Their 1978 study revealed that it is important for a person not to have a "searching" look, if she want to maintain her credibility. This means that she should not lower her eyes or avoid eye contact too frequently. Likewise, she must not blink or move her eyelids too much.

In his extensive 1986 study into eye behavior, Kleine Kerk documented the significant impact that eye contact can have in helping to establish credibility and therefore in convincing others. He emphasized that numerous empirical studies support the stereotypical belief that we are more inclined to trust people who look us straight in the eye, whereas people who avoid eye contact are more easily labeled as liars. This explains, for example, why witnesses in court who avoid looking at the cross-examining lawyers are less likely to be believed. It also explains why people in airports who avoid eye contact with security personnel are more rather than less likely to be stopped and searched.

In 1987, Hornik further confirmed that the powers of persuasion of a person who maintains eye contact with the person he wants to persuade are greater than if he avoids eye contact too frequently. Other convincing documentation that direct eye contact is interpreted as a sign of credibility in social relationships was provided by Burgoon and Saine in 1978 and Burgoon, Coker, and Coker in 1986. Direct eye contact can have a positive influence on both the perception and the effective communication of credibility.

When someone looks into our eyes as she talks to us, it gives the impression of honesty. If she avoids eye contact, her message seems less congruent and we may start to doubt her sincerity.

A similar conclusion was reached by Burgoon, Manusov, Mineo, and Hale in 1985. They noted that the avoidance of eye contact during interviews made candidates seem less credible, thereby emphasizing that the negative connotations associated with averted eyes and the possible painful consequences this might involve are interpreted as a negative form of nonverbal behavior.

The behavior of the eyes plays a key role in the establishment, maintenance, and termination of interpersonal relations. In 1989, Malandro, Barker, and Gaut concluded that the type of eye contact can be a signal of the kind of interaction that is possible between two people, or a predictor of how this interaction will develop. Eye contact displays the interest you have in another person and gives that person the opportunity to gather information about you and your intentions. In particular, eye contact is indicative of the likely level of intimacy of a contact, much more than many other gestures and nonverbal signals.

According to Webbink in 1986, reciprocated eye contact expresses much more than the language of other parts of the body and indicates a frank openness between two people. In general, it is possible to say that the longer the eye contact is maintained, the more intense the level of intimacy becomes. Returning someone else's eye contact in the same way plays a key role in the majority of human interactions and is part of a process that is necessary for strengthening a mutual feeling of participation, and therefore intimacy.

Argyle was similarly convinced of the primary importance of the information communicated to others by the eyes. His research, published in 1988, concluded that this information is particularly valuable for deciphering and interpreting incongruent messages. This dominant role of eye contact in recognizing incongruence was further underlined in 1989 by Burgoon, Buller, and Woodall, who spoke of "the priority of eye contact" above other nonverbal signals, while conceding that this priority was apparent in some circumstances and not others.

Research by Fujimoto in 1992 additionally established that eye contact, assisted by other facial expressions, is the dominant source of information for assessing the emotional content of a message. When the words and the eye signals of a person communicate contradictory information about the emotions being experienced, eye contact is the more reliable of the two sources.

All the above research confirmed the world-famous findings originally published in 1981 by Mehrabian, who claimed that just 7 percent of our communication is expressed in words, while some 55 percent is conveyed by our body language. Although the precise figures were later modified by Mehrabian and other scientists, it remains indisputable that the majority of our messages to others are transmitted by body language.

This was in keeping with the results of the tests conducted in 1979 by De Paulo and Rosenthal, when participants chose information received via visual channels as being more reliable than all other channels for assessing the truth of a message. In other words, if you need to choose between a person's words and their body language, always opt for the body language if you want to know the truth.

SUMMARY	
Staring	Desire for confrontation, sexual interest
Avoiding eye contact	Uncertainty, shyness, something to hide
The length of eye contact	Eye contact for 60 to 80 percent of the time creates confidence
Larger pupils	Interest, positive emotions, possibly fear
Smaller pupils	Lack of interest, negative emotions
Large eyes	Amazement
Quick exchange of glances	Exchange of information
Angry look	Displeasure, superiority, contempt
Winking	Attracting attention, warning
Confirmatory blinking	Confirmation, agreement
Sideways glance	Disbelief, reluctance, distrust, disapproval
Narrowing the eyes	Request for more information, concentration, anger
Blinking with your eyes	Fast blinking necessary after intensive thinking
Averting your gaze	Hiding something, needing distance
Raising your eyebrows	Surprise, greeting
Raising one eyebrow	Disbelief
Lowering your eyebrows	Dissatisfaction, anger, or unpleasant surprise

SUMMARY (cont.)	
Pursed lips	Lack of acceptance, not wanting to say something
Real smile	Contraction of orbicularis oculi (eye corners stretched, eyebrows lowered)
False smile	Only with the mouth

7

Microexpressions: The Dead Giveaways

IN THIS CHAPTER, YOU'LL DISCOVER:

- The most reliable indicators of what people are feeling
- How involuntary muscle movements reveal emotions
  like happiness, disapproval, and even contempt

Microexpressions are a special category of facial expressions, which have been the subject of considerable and specific scientific research during the past fifty years. We define microexpressions as subtle muscular movements in the face with a duration of half a second or less. Microexpressions often occur unconsciously and reflect emotions that we are feeling at that particular moment. If you compare the face to a screen, the brain is the projector of our emotions, which cause our facial muscles to contract for just a brief instant.

There are seven basic emotions that are shown in the same way in the face in all cultures. Research conducted among blind people has proven that microexpressions are not culturally learned, but are a biological phenomenon which each of us is equipped with from birth. They are the physical reaction to the way our brain translates emotional impulses. What's more, most people are unable to control these unconscious contractions of the muscles, because they are directly generated by the emotions.

Microexpressions display most of the basic emotions. Robert Plutchik was the first to develop the theory of eight basic emotions: sorrow, dislike, anger, fear, anticipation, pleasure, acceptance, and surprise. He even developed a specific graphic in color for each emotion to reflect the fact that they could be combined to create new emotions; for example, fear + surprise = alarm or pleasure + fear = guilt. Since it was not possible to observe anticipation and acceptance as a universal code visible in the face, the only positive emotion that remained in Plutchik's theory was pleasure, later more commonly referred to as happiness. This term covers a whole family of positive emotions, including acceptance, anticipation, approval, pleasure, and joy.

Today, microexpressions are grouped into seven basic and universal emotions: anger, dislike, fear, surprise, happiness, sadness, and contempt.

What we now refer to as microexpressions were first identified in the nineteenth century by Duchenne de Boulogne, a famous French neurologist. He combined his huge knowledge of facial anatomy with his passion for photography and his expertise in the use of electricity to stimulate individual muscles in the face. He recorded his conclusion in his book *The Mechanism of Human Facial Expression*, published in 1862.

The second person to write about microexpressions was Charles Darwin in *The Expression of the Emotions in Man and Animals*, published in 1872. Darwin noted the universal nature of facial expressions and listed the muscles that were used to generate them. In the findings of their 1966 study,

Haggard and Isaacs reported how they had been able to observe "micro-moment facial expressions" when examining films of psychotherapy sessions, initially searching for signals of nonverbal communication between therapists and their patients. Ekman and Friesen conducted numerous investigations into facial expressions and were eventually able to confirm that seven basic emotions are displayed facially in the same manner in twenty-one different cultures.

In 1960, William S. Condon conducted pioneering research into interactions that last for fractions of a second. He reduced his groundbreaking conclusions to a film fragment lasting just four and a half seconds. Each of the constituent images he had analyzed and recorded lasted for just 1/25 of a second. After having examined this film fragment minutely for eighteen months, he reported on what he called "interactional micro-movements"; for example, how a woman raised her shoulder at almost exactly the same moment as a man raised his hand. According to Condon, this interplay of micro-movements in combination with each other made possible a series of micro-rhythms.

Paul Ekman's later research into emotions and their relationship to facial expressions took Darwin's work to a higher level and proved beyond question that certain emotion-related facial expressions are not culturally determined, but are biological in origin. These expressions are universal and transcend cultures. On the basis of his work, in 1976 Ekman developed his Facial Action Coding System (FACS) with Wallace V. Freisen. FACS is a system for classifying human facial expressions and is still used today by psychologists, researchers, and animators.

In this chapter, we look at the most common variations of three of the seven basic emotions, which can occur regularly in day-to-day conversation. If you have already had microexpression training, you will notice that our approach to identifying and interpreting short muscular movements in the face is designed to make things as simple as possible. This is because we refer to all facial expressions of half a second or less by the generic term microexpressions, even though from a purely scientific perspective some of them can better be described as partial expressions, subtle expressions, or masked expressions. While there are slight differences between the different types of partial, subtle, and masked expressions, our focus in this book is on applying accepted scientific conclusions to daily practice.

Neutral Face

THE NEUTRAL FACE IS YOUR BASIS FOR COMPARISON.

It is important to be able to identify when someone is wearing a neutral face, because this gives you a basis for comparing or noticing the difference when the facial microexpressions activated by emotions kick in. Sometimes, wearing a neutral face may express the fact that the person is experiencing no emotions at that particular moment or has no opinion about what she is hearing. In such situations, it can be useful to check if she is really paying attention to what you are saying. It is always possible that she is simply not listening to you or has not properly heard what you said.

You have probably experienced when someone deliberately puts on a poker face. Most of us are capable of producing our own variant of this, when necessary. For this reason, it is important to be able to make a distinction between a neutral face and a poker face. A neutral face will appear more relaxed and more spontaneous than a poker face. With a poker face, you often get the impression that the person concerned is wearing a mask. The muscles in the face are more tensed and you can notice that the person is deliberately trying to suppress reactions to what is happening around him. He will not answer questions spontaneously, but will first take time to think about how he wants to respond, while at the same time attempting not to react with his face.

This is also the reason why people with something to hide often wear dark sunglasses, so that people cannot see part of their face and, in particular, their eyes.

Happiness: Corners of the Mouth Turned Up

You can read happiness in someone's face when both corners of their mouth are turned up symmetrically to the same level. If you can recognize it, this microexpression is extremely useful in everyday life. For example, if I ask my partner what she wants to do tonight,

BOTH CORNERS OF THE MOUTH
TURNED UP INDICATE HAPPINESS.

"Shall we meet up with friends, stay at home, or go to the movies?" and if I see both corners of her mouth turn up when I mention *friends*, then I know that she has already made her nonverbal choice.

Compare This with a Real, Wholehearted Smile of Joy

This is not a microexpression, but we show it as an example, so that you can see the difference between a microexpression that lasts for half a second or less and a macroexpression that lasts for significantly longer. The photo is also useful to see the difference between a real and a false smile.

When you see the orbicularis oculi (the muscle around the eye) contract, you know that you are looking at a real smile, a so-called Duchenne smile. The contraction of the orbicularis oculi muscles makes the areas of skin between the eyes and the outer edge of the eyebrows stretch and lower slightly, often accompanied by the slight low-

THIS IS NOT A MICROEXPRESSION.

ering of the eyebrows as well. These two movements are a reliable indicator that someone is experiencing pleasure in the left prefrontal cortex of their brain, so that the happiness they are expressing is genuine.

HOW GOOD ARE PEOPLE AT RECOGNIZING MICROEXPRESSIONS?

The average score when people first do a microexpression test is just 24.09 percent (based on 2,664 unique test results worldwide in 2012). Fewer than 12 percent achieve a score of more than 50 percent. This leads to the conclusion that in their daily conversations most people pay little attention to microexpressions, or else they are not aware of the significance of these small muscular contractions, which are nevertheless the most reliable indicators of the way people are feeling.

The average score of people who have completed a course of microexpression training is 89.45 percent. In our studies in various companies, we have found a clear correlation between sales results and the ability of sales staff to identify microexpressions. It has repeatedly been shown that the best salespeople have a natural talent for spotting and reacting appropriately to these expressions. What's more, it is a talent they have often acquired unconsciously. Are you curious to know whether or not you are any good at identifying microexpressions? Have a go at the free test on www.MicroExpressionsTest.com. You will know your score within two minutes.

❝ The best salespeople are excellent at reading body language. ❞

Happiness

In behavioral science, the term *happiness* is used as a generic description for the whole family of positive emotions, including acceptance, anticipation, approval, pleasure, confirmation, and excitement. Happiness is the most attractive emotion. We like to be surrounded by laughing people and we are prepared to make those around us feel happy and comfortable in return. We often smile or laugh to show that we agree with someone, or that we like them, or in the hope that they will like us.

The microexpression of happiness is a crucial signal in business contexts, especially if you want to know whether your conversation partner agrees with your proposal or not. Consequently, it is important to know how you can recognize this emotional signal. One complication is the fact that it is easy to mistake the micro-expression for happiness with the microexpression for contempt. Both are very similar, with the exception that the expression for contempt is asymmetrical, while the expression for happiness is symmetrical. When people experience pleasure, both the corners of the mouth are turned up. When they experience contempt, only one corner (it doesn't matter which one) is turned up. Contempt has a totally different meaning from happiness; it is an expression of superiority. If someone displays contempt during a business meeting, it almost certainly means that she does not appreciate your proposal or that she thinks she knows better than you do.

Contempt can be shown immediately before or immediately after a smile. This is designed to mask the expression of contempt, but it can still be seen for just a fraction of a second within the smile. It is essential to be able to distinguish between these two different facial movements; if you confuse them, your negotiations are unlikely to lead to a successful conclusion.

Contempt

In behavioral science, the term *contempt* is used as a generic description for the whole family of negative emotions, including superiority, sarcasm, "I-know-better," and dominance. Contempt is the only one of the seven basic emotions that is clearly asymmetrical in its expression. It looks as though you are smiling to yourself, because only one of the two corners of your mouth is raised. In reality, it is not a smile, but rather a sign that you feel superior to others around you. It is an expression that is used after someone has had the chance to compare their knowledge and experience with that of someone else, and has reached the conclusion that theirs are better.

People who are inclined to show contempt will be more ready to assess and judge others and express negative thoughts about them. If you see contempt on your conversation partner's face during a business meeting, you would be well advised to change your line of argument, since you have obviously not been able to convince him so far. For example, you can offer more examples to support your case, or reemphasize your own level of expertise and experience, or ask questions that will make clear the reasons for his resistance. If someone shows you this contemptuous expression before you have even said a word, you can expect the conversation to be a difficult one. In certain circumstances, the same expression can also be an indication of pride.

Contempt: One Corner of the Mouth Turned Up

THIS WILL BE A DIFFICULT CUSTOMER.

You can read contempt on someone's face when she feels superior or when she regards someone else as inferior. This microexpression is easy to recognize, because it is the only one of the seven basic emotions that is displayed asymmetrically: only one of the two corners of the mouth is turned up.

Contempt During a Smile

You can also recognize contempt during a smile when one of the corners of the mouth is raised more quickly or further than the other, or comes down again more slowly.

NOT A SMILE, BUT CONTEMPT

Dislike

In behavioral science, the term *dislike* is used as a generic description for a whole family of negative emotions, ranging from modest disapproval to outright rejection and disgust. This is the expression you make when you open the fridge door and discover that your milk has gone sour. There will be wrinkles visible in your face, because you will have turned up your upper lip. This is an automatic reaction to a bad smell, and represents an attempt to close off the nasal passages as far as possible.

During the evolutionary process, this facial expression helped people of the same tribe to protect each other from the harmful consequences of rotten food. Nowadays, it has become an expression to show that we don't like someone or do not agree with what we are hearing. If your customer shows this sign of disapproval during your negotiations, this will mean that your proposal was not as good as you thought. By being able to notice the expression quickly, you will have the opportunity to steer the conversation in a different direction before it is too late, perhaps by asking exploratory questions or putting forward new arguments. In some circumstances, it can also save you time, if you can see early in a conversation that the customer has no interest at all in what you are trying to say.

THE MICROEXPRESSIONS OF MILLIONAIRES

Many people regard millionaires as cold people who seldom show their emotions. It is certainly true that millionaires are generally knowledgeable and self-confident, so that their body language displays the fact that they are not to be trifled with. Even so, studies have revealed that in most cases millionaires are highly empathic. For example, there is a video of Patryk's live conversation with multimillionaire Roland Duchatelet on RTBF, the French-language TV station in Belgium. When we analyze what Duchatelet does with his face while he is talking, we see that his facial expressions support his words in a sympathetic manner. There is a clear congruence and it is obvious that this is not just a poker face.

> As already mentioned in Chapter 1, this kind of empathic expressivity supports good contact with others. This can offer important benefits at key moments during negotiations, because your conversation partners will feel understood.

Dislike: Wrinkles Around the Nose

Dislike is easy to identify from the wrinkles it creates around the nose. These wrinkles appear because the upper lip is tensed and slightly raised up. The lower lip can also be slightly raised.

WRINKLES AROUND THE NOSE MEAN DISLIKE.

Dislike: Upper Lip Turned Up

A clear sign of dislike is the turning up of the upper lip. In this variation of the expression, the teeth are also visible. Note that the wrinkles around the nose are still visible. Wrinkles around the nose nearly always signify dislike.

THIS DOES NOT SMELL (OR SOUND) GOOD.

Expressions of Fear, Anger, Sadness, and Surprise

So far in this book, we have not discussed in detail the micro-expressions of fear, anger, sadness, and surprise. Each of these expressions have many more variations than the three other emotions we have just examined. Below you can find a single and commonly occurring expression for each emotion to serve as an example:

- **FEAR:** the lips stretched horizontally sideways
- **ANGER:** the eyes narrowed and the eyebrows pulled down
- **SADNESS:** the inner edges of the eyebrows raised
- **SURPRISE:** the eyebrows tensed and raised, together with the upper eyelids

FEAR   ANGER   SADNESS   SURPRISE

SUMMARY	
Happiness	Both corners of the mouth turned up
Contempt	One corner of the mouth turned up
Dislike	Wrinkles around the nose
Anger	Lips stretched horizontally sideways
Fear	Eyes narrowed and eyebrows pulled down
Sadness	Inner edges of eyebrows raised
Surprise	Eyebrows tensed and raised, together with upper eyelids

8

Decisionmaking Body Language

In this chapter, we will focus on the decisive body language that can be crucial to your negotiating success. When I (Kasia) was twelve years old, I started accompanying my stepfather on many of his business trips and was present at many business lunches. He was the owner of a large construction company specialized in office buildings. Together we visited many different Western and Arab lands.

Observing him over the course of many meetings, I noticed how my stepfather's decisions were revealed on his face long before he spoke them. One time I watched him negotiate a price for an expensive silver vase. When the price he offered was good, he showed contempt with one lip up, when the fee was too low he showed disgust with the wrinkles around the nose and then anger. With practice, I was often able to predict the outcome of these meetings before either party had made it clear.

In this chapter, you will also find a description of our BLINK Conversation Technique™, which will help you to steer conversations in such a way that you will receive all the information you want to know without ever saying a word about it.

In short, this chapter contains vital guidance that can be used beneficially in many different kinds of business situations, including sales, recruitment, and negotiation.

> **" If the chin-rubbing stops, the decision has often already been made. "**

Rubbing the Chin

If someone massages his chin, this means that he is usually assessing a situation. This gesture also indicates that the person is

getting ready to make a decision. If the chin rubbing stops, the decision has often already been made. Consequently, it is important to take the right action while the rubbing is still in progress. If the person turns his head or glances to one side during the massaging process, this generally means that he is positive toward what

THINKING, ASSESSING (LOOKING UP OR DOWN GENERALLY NEGATIVE, LOOKING TO ONE SIDE GENERALLY POSITIVE)

has been proposed. If he looks upward or downward, this generally means that his reaction will be unfavorable. In this latter case, you should say something or ask a question before he actually speaks his final judgment. By breaking his train of negative thought in this way, you might still have the opportunity to persuade him in a more positive direction.

Eyelids Lowered with the Index Finger on Lips

Another gesture that can precede the making of a decision is the lowering of the upper eyelids and the placing of the index finger against the lips. This indicates that the person is thinking about a particular subject and does not want to be disturbed. Whether or not you decide to disturb her anyway will depend on whether you think her thoughts are positive or negative. If this position was preceded by largely negative body language, you have nothing to lose by interrupting with a question or a new and more convincing line of argument.

DO NOT DISTURB, A DECISION IS BEING MADE.

Glasses in the Mouth

You have probably noticed that some people who wear glasses have a tendency to take them off at crucial moments and put part of them—usually one of the arms—into their mouth. Others may

A DECISION IS BEING MADE.

simply wave their glasses about, with a concentrated look on their face. In both cases, the person concerned is getting ready to make a decision. As with the gestures already discussed, your reaction will best be determined by the general impression conveyed by the person's body language, both during the preceding minutes and during this moment of reflection: Is it positive or negative?

Putting Objects in the Mouth

We have already seen that putting objects in your mouth is a sign of uncertainty. If you notice this action while someone is making a decision, it is a nonverbal signal that the person needs more specific arguments or details before they can make a well-founded decision. If you fail to answer this nonverbal question, there is a chance that their uncertainty will gain the upper hand, so that the result will be negative.

UNCERTAINTY, MORE DETAILS NEEDED

Hands in a Pyramid

In Chapter 3, we saw that joining your fingers in the form of a pyramid can be seen as a sign of self-confidence and dominance. Within the context of decisionmaking, it shows that the person is convinced of the wisdom of his own opinion. If the decision is likely to be favorable to you will depend on the other nonverbal signals you have picked up in the course of the conversation. If his body language was positive immediately before assuming the pyramid position, this is the ideal moment to sign a contract or make a definite agreement.

If his preceding body language was negative, your chances are slim. All you can do is interrupt his train of thought and try to move the conversation in a different direction, perhaps before returning to the original subject at a later stage with more convincing arguments. If the person with the pyramid hands also leans his head back, this signifies a superior and dominant attitude. It will be very difficult to persuade this person in your favor, unless the initiative comes from his side. This position makes a positive conversation difficult, since it indicates he is not really listening to what you say.

**SOMEONE WHO IS
CERTAIN OF HIS OPINION**

Hands Behind the Head

As with the pyramid hands, a person who puts her hands behind her head is displaying self-confidence and dominance. It is important to be aware of the timing of this gesture and the other signals that accompany it. Interpreting the different possible meanings of the gesture, as discussed in Chapter 3, will help you to decide your best strategy.

Leaning the Body Forward

If your conversation partner leans her upper body forward, this is generally a good sign. It probably means that she agrees with you, is interested in your proposal, and is open for further collaboration. However, if the position is combined with other negative body language, it can mean that she is preparing for confrontation.

INTEREST, READY FOR CONFRONTATION

Crossed Arms and Head Leaned Back

If your negotiating partner answers your proposal with a closed body position with folded arms and his head leaned back, his

answer is certain to be no. In these circumstances, it is better not to persist, since this will simply strengthen his decision. All you can do is try a different angle of approach in the hope that this may help him to reach a different conclusion later on.

REFUSAL, DENIAL

Nodding with Crossed Arms and a Smile

This position needs to be interpreted with care, depending on the moment and context of its use. When not meant sarcastically, nodding the head with a smile is a good sign. The addition of the crossed arms can mean that the person first needs a little time and distance to think, either because the decision is not a simple one or because they do not want to show too much enthusiasm. In any event, it is still a positive gesture.

HIDDEN ENTHUSIASM OR SARCASM

The Positioning of the Body and Feet

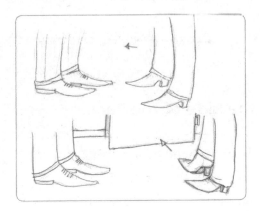

**INDICATION OF
WHERE ATTENTION IS FOCUSED**

As already mentioned, the direction in which the body is pointing, perhaps confirmed by the direction of the feet, is a good indication of where a person's attention is focused. In general, these parts of the body will be aimed at the person with whom the person feels most empathy or interest.

Nodding the Head

If your conversation partner regularly nods her head, without accompanying the motion with other more negative body language, this means that she agrees with you. If she does not agree with you, she will more likely avoid eye contact or support her head with her hand. It can also be useful to nod encouragingly,

particularly at the start of conversation, since this will stimulate the other person to talk more freely. The more you know, the easier it is to bridge the initial distance between you and maintain good contact.

HIDDEN ENTHUSIASM OR SARCASM

Hand on the Side of the Face

If someone places his hand or index finger on his cheek or along the side of his face without actually supporting the head, this is another good sign, since it demonstrates interest and a desire to listen to what you have to say.

INTEREST

NEGATIVE BODY LANGUAGE
DURING THE DECISIONMAKING PROCESS

The negative positions and gestures we discussed in Chapter 4 can also be used to indicate a negative response or attitude in the negotiating and decisionmaking process. In this context, some of these movements and gestures have an additional emphasis:

- A severe look: critical thoughts.
- Hands on knees and body leaned forward: ready to leave
- Head held back: superiority, desire to end the conversation
- Balled fists: anger, resistance, aggression
- Hands in pockets: resistance, concealing an opinion, maintaining distance
- Hand on the mouth while thinking: reflection, assessing with interest
- Playing with objects: lack of interest, thoughts elsewhere, nervousness
- Supporting the head: boredom, lack of interest

Supporting the Head

If the hand or one or more fingers are used to support the head, this signifies that your conversation partner is starting to get bored.

BOREDOM, LACK OF INTEREST

You often see this gesture during long meetings or uninspired speeches. Even just supporting the chin with the thumb can be interpreted as negative and critical. If you do nothing to adjust your arguments when you see this position, the situation will most likely soon turn to your disadvantage.

Clearing Up

READY TO LEAVE

If a person has not done this before and if a moment occurs in the conversation which makes it possible, the sudden gathering together of papers or a quick rummaging in a briefcase may signal a desire to bring the conversation to a close.

Elbows on the Arms of Your Chair

We have already mentioned that self-confident people have no qualms about occupying their space. Placing your arms on or

FEELING COMFORTABLE

over the arms of your chair shows that you feel comfortable and that you probably expect to have the last word about any decision that needs to be made. You can also use this gesture when you feel that too little attention is being given to you in situations involving a number of people.

Jacket Open

When one of the participants in a negotiation opens the button of his jacket, this is a positive sign. Providing the temperature in the room has remained the same, it means that the other person is becoming more convinced about your arguments or is ready to work with you. According to Nierenberg and Calero in 2002, this is one of the signals that indicate the positive evolution of a conversation. This applies equally to other gestures, such as moving closer to your conversation partner or uncrossing your legs: All are indications that possible resistance is being weakened.

OPENNESS

Rubbing the Back of the Neck

FRUSTRATION

If someone rubs the back of her head or neck with her hand, this is a sign of frustration. It means that the conversation is not moving in the right direction and that she does not know how best to escape from the difficult situation in which she finds herself. Perhaps this frustration has its origin in a price that is too high. Or perhaps the person has not been able to fulfill a commitment she made previously. If a colleague makes this gesture when you ask her about something she had promised to do, there is a good chance that the task will not be completed on time and that she feels guilty about it.

The Pistol

AGGRESSION

If someone brings together his index fingers and points them in a forward direction, the symbolism is clear. The nonverbal aggression in this pistol-like gesture is plain for all to see.

Rubbing the Hands Together

We rub our hands together when a decision is made and we are getting ready to take action. It is as if we want to warm up our hands before carrying out our intentions accurately and energetically. However, the same gesture can also indicate happiness or even malicious pleasure, depending on the speed with which it is implemented (as explained in Chapter 5).

**WARMING UP
FOR ACTION
(UNLESS SLOW)**

Tapping with Your Fingers on the Back of Your Other Hand

We have already learned that tapping with your fingers is a sign of nervousness. But if you tap with the fingers of one hand on the back of your other hand, this signifies additionally that you are nervous about doing something or are waiting for something to occur.

NERVOUSNESS

Pressing on Your Finger Pads

When someone massages the inside of the palm of her other hand with her thumb, this suggests that she finds herself in a difficult situation—for example, when she does not want to commit

herself further in a matter that has turned out differently from what she had expected.

DIFFICULT SITUATION

Hands Relaxed Over Each Other

If this gesture is not simply a habit of the person concerned, it may indicate his desire to distance himself from the situation or to withdraw from the current conversation—although this is dependent on the timing, context, and speed with which the hands are folded over each other. In some circumstances, it can also be a more positive signal: for example, after a good meal, when the person wants to show that he feels comfortable and wishes to relax for a few moments.

MAINTAINING DISTANCE, RELAXATION

Both Hands Against the Head

INFORMATION OVERLOAD

This gesture can mean that the person feels overwhelmed with new information. Equally, it can also be a sign of tiredness or reluctance. The correct interpretation will probably become clear through its combination with other gestures.

Indications of Lying

A British research project established that on average we tell four relatively major lies each day. Two independent American studies came to the conclusion that we also each hear roughly two hundred lies a day told by others.

Even so, in our opinion it is not a good idea to begin a business discussion with the intention of detecting your conversation partner's lies. This kind of attitude would lead to very few positive results, because it makes it very difficult to build up a positive relationship. Our experience in the business world suggests that the number of people who tell truly serious lies with malicious intent is relatively small. The idea is to avoid damaging situations of this kind and make sure you don't make yourself an easy target for the inveterate liars. However, there are, a number of gray zones where interpretation needs to be made carefully:

- People who fail to do what they promised on time, but always come up with new, rational, and relevant excuses for their failure
- People who highlight their capacities and experience selectively, in order to create a better impression
- People who try to ask a higher price in mid-project
- People who unexpectedly no longer wish to cooperate, but without explaining why

This kind of behavior may not be lying in terms of the criminal code; it is more a question of white lies, which, like it or not, are an integral part of doing business. The way you define a lie and the attention you devote to it can also have an impact on the way you interpret nonverbal signals. For example, some people automatically assume that others will lie. As a result, they may focus on a small number of gestures taken out of context that support their preconceived hypothesis, while ignoring the wider and more important picture. We do not intend to discuss here whether or not failing to disclose something with the best of intentions can (or should be) regarded as a lie. In the final analysis, everyone must decide for themselves what lies they are prepared to accept in the gray areas that will always exist.

We recommend not focusing too heavily on lies, white or not, but concentrating instead on finding the best way to work together with your business partners. It is better to spend time searching for ways to collaborate, based on common goals and mutual understanding, rather than approaching each discussion as though you are some kind of human lie detector. A good knowledge of body language will help you to find better business partners and interpret their behavior and words.

In everyday relationships, many of the people we encounter transmit unclear and inconsistent messages, perhaps to manipulate their environment, perhaps to achieve a sense of control, or perhaps to persuade us to pay a higher price than is really necessary. In these circumstances, it is essential to be able to detect the incongruencies between their words and their body language, so that we can take correct and concrete decisions that serve our own best interests, rather than theirs. If we suspect that someone is trying to hide something from us, it is useful to have a list of basic gestures and positions that we can look for to identify these possible incongruencies. If carried out shortly after each other, the following gestures should alert you to the fact that someone may be trying to pull the wool over your eyes:

- Covering the mouth (not wanting to say something)
- Touching the end of the nose (nervousness and/or stress)
- Rubbing the eyes (not wanting to see something)
- Stepping back or adopting a defensive posture (keeping distance)
- Winning time by using objects as a barrier (keeping distance)
- Sudden changes of behavior when a suspect subject is discussed
- Renewed body tension when that subject is raised again

NOT WANTING TO SAY SOMETHING

NERVOUSNESS

NOT WANTING TO SEE SOMETHING

KEEPING DISTANCE

At this point, we once again need to debunk the myth that certain gestures, movements, or expressions can betray lying. The body language signals referred to above are only indications that may suggest the experiencing of certain emotions that may or may not be connected with lying. What's more, these signals are among the weakest indicators for detecting untruths. They are only of value in combination with other indicators, taking account of the normal behavior of the person concerned and following careful application of the five basic principles of body language interpretation. Only then can you conclude that someone is lying. Probably.

When you suspect someone of lying and notice that they seem to be experiencing fear, even this is not confirmation that they are definitely lying. The emotion of fear does not necessarily indicate that the person is afraid of being caught. Perhaps she is simply afraid of not being believed. And the reverse is also true; an absence of fear does not inevitably mean that she is not lying. In order to establish accurately whether someone is lying or not takes years of practice and experience, in which a number of important rules must always be followed.

The Golden Rules for Detecting Lies

All the gestures, movements, positions, and expressions in this book can be an indication of a lie, if they contradict what you hear. The golden rule is to find and identify the incongruencies between the signals you receive from a person's body language and the message you receive from their words. These incongruencies can take one of the following forms, among others:

- The body language is positive; the words are negative
- The body language is positive; the words are neutral
- The body language is negative; the words are positive
- The body language is negative; the words are neutral

To establish correctly whether or not someone is lying, it is necessary to learn how to apply all the signs and signals described in this book. The accurate interpretation of nonverbal communication demands a great deal of practice and theoretical preparation, if you wish to avoid making painful mistakes, such as accusing people who never had any intention of lying or concealing something from you. As you acquire these skills, always remember the golden rule: If there is incongruence between a person's words and their body language, body language never lies.

❝ Body language never lies. ❞

The most reliable signals for detecting lies are the signals emitted by emotions that are difficult to suppress or falsify, because their outward physical expression is completely unconscious. Yet even here we need to be careful with our interpretations, because they are not signals of lies per se, but of increased stress. These difficult-to-conceal signals include intensive sweating, faster breathing, blushing, tears, a faster heart rate, and microexpressions. The advantage of being able to accurately identify microexpressions is that they are universal and clearly reflect just one of the seven basic emotions. What's more, they are directly activated by the body's limbic system, so that they are very difficult to mask or control.

Paying Careful Attention Always Works Best

If your conversation partner lies or deliberately conceals or withholds information from you, matters have probably already gone too far to build up and maintain a good relationship. For this reason, it is important from your very first meeting to create a positive framework in which authentic communication can flourish. The best way to ensure success and to secure a positive reaction during the decisionmaking process involves the following elements:

- Pay careful attention to the body language of your conversation partner and reflect his nonverbal behavior during the first fifteen minutes of your conversation. The other person will immediately feel well understood and will positively experience your empathy for him.

- Prevent your conversation partner from announcing negative decisions by reacting quickly and proactively to the body language that you see her display. Many of the gestures, movements, positions, and expressions described in Chapters 4 to 8 will allow you to notice when someone disagrees with you. Try to use this knowledge to your benefit.

■ Remember that you always have some room for maneuvering to change your conversation partner's opinion, as long as he has not yet confirmed this opinion verbally, even if the response of his body language to your own opinion was initially unfavorable. As long as he does not translate his thoughts and emotions into words, you can try to convince him to the contrary.

BLINK Conversation Technique™: Getting Answers Without Asking Questions

As we've shown, it's very useful to have a good knowledge of body language, so that you can better understand what your conversation partner is really feeling. The next step is to learn how you can best use this valuable knowledge within the conversation. The fact that you might have seen a microexpression of disgust in response to your question only gives you limited information about the emotion the other person is experiencing. How you react to this signal can influence the rest of the conversation. You can hardly say to someone: "I see disgust in your face: why is that?" It is seldom a good idea to confront someone directly with this kind of information.

So how do you get answers to these questions that are difficult to ask? How do you get the information you need that the other person cannot or will not give in words? The solution is to be found in the BLINK Conversation Technique™, known as BLINK for short. We developed this technique so that we can obtain the information we need without having to ask any questions about it.

This is particularly useful at crucial moments in a conversation, such as discussing the right price or when you notice incongruence between what you are hearing and what you are seeing. BLINK stands for Body Language Interpretations Nominology Know-how. It is a system of verbal strategies that will help you in a diplomatic manner to explore difficult subjects for your conversation partner, with the aim of continuing your collaboration in the future.

BLINK can also help you in situations where you are not certain about your interpretation, by allowing you to learn more about your conversation partner without asking questions that might generate resistance. A good example of the value of BLINK is the case of a manager who dealt regularly with salespeople. His problem was that he could not recognize the microexpression of contempt when a salesperson sat next to him, so that he could only see half of his face. From this position, what seemed like a microexpression of contempt might actually be an expression of happiness. Thanks to BLINK, he could easily check which of these two possibilities was correct.

> **" Body language gives you answers without the need to ask explicit questions. "**

The basic principle of BLINK consists of formulating your words in such a way that you trigger certain emotional reactions in your conversation partner, so that you can discover the answers you need from her body language. For example, instead of directly asking a job candidate what salary she expects to receive (a question for which she will probably have prepared an answer), it is a better idea to tell her what the standard salary is for the job she is interested in and see how she reacts. If you can formulate and communicate your story in this way, her body language will tell you whether the salary she expects is higher or lower than the figure you have mentioned.

The strength of this technique lies in the fact that when we are listening we have a natural tendency to unconsciously show with our body language whether we agree or disagree with what is being said. It is easier to lie or withhold information when we are speaking, because speech is usually something we consciously prepare in advance. It is much more difficult to do this when we are required to listen, certainly if your conversation partner is a body language expert.

We are now entering the fascinating world of "body language for specialists." It will often happen that you do not get the information you need just from what you see. Many times, the most valuable information is gleaned from what you don't see, from the gestures the other person doesn't make. This can tell you just as much about what the person is feeling.

&& It is not only what you see, but also what you don't see that gives you the information you need. 99

It should be evident that this technique can be useful in many different business situations, such as sales discussions or contract negotiations. For example, instead of asking your customer which of the advantages you offer is most important to her, you can simply summarize these advantages and watch carefully how her body language reacts to each advantage you name. This will show you where you need to focus your attention and what kind of arguments you should use to maximize your chance of convincing her to place an order.

By following a number of basic rules (and with lots of practice), you should be able to gather all the information you need without your conversation partner ever being aware of it. If applied correctly, it can even help to create a positive atmosphere for your discussions, since it avoids the need for asking difficult questions and gives the other person the feeling that you understand her and know what she values.

A first simple exercise to explore the power of BLINK is to suggest to your partner a list of things that you might like to do this weekend. In this initial phase, it is important NOT to ask any questions, but simply to offer a few notification sentences. You might say something like: "We could go for a drink, or take in a film, or visit a friend, or just stay at home and watch TV." While you are speaking, your partner's body language will betray their preference.

❝ While you speak, their body language will give you the answer you need. ❞

SUMMARY	
Rubbing the chin	Thinking, assessing (looking up or down generally negative, looking to one side generally positive)
Eyelid lowered with the index finger on lips	Do not disturb, a decision is being made
Glasses in the mouth	A decision is being made
Putting objects in the mouth	Uncertainty, more details needed
Hands in a pyramid	Someone who is certain of his opinion
Hands behind the head	Arrogance
Leaning the body forward	Interest, ready for confrontation
Crossed arms and head leaned back	Refusal, denial
Nodding with crossed arms and a smile	Hidden enthusiasm or sarcasm
Positioning of the body and feet	Indication of where attention is focused
Nodding the head	Agreement
Hand on the side of your face	Interest
Supporting the head	Boredom, lack of interest
Clearing up	Ready to leave
Elbows on the arms of your chair	Feeling comfortable
Jacket open	Openness
Rubbing the back of the neck	Frustration
The pistol	Aggression

SUMMARY (cont.)	
Rubbing the hands together	Warming up for action (unless slow)
Tapping with your fingers on the back of the other hand	Nervousness
Pressing on your finger pads	Difficult situation
Hands relaxed over each other	Maintaining distance, relaxation
Both hands against the head	Information overload
Covering the mouth	Not wanting to say something
Touching the end of the nose	Nervousness, stress
Rubbing the eyes	Not wanting to see something
Stepping back or adopting a defensive posture	Keeping distance
Winning time by using objects	Keeping distance
Sweating	Increased stress
Faster breathing	Increased stress
Blushing	Increased stress
Faster heart rate	Increased stress

9

Practice Exercises

In this chapter, you will find a number of sample situations in which body language needs to be interpreted. The drawings are literal applications of the gestures, movements, positions, expressions, and interpretations that have been examined earlier in the book. As a practice exercise, we suggest that you first write down your complete interpretation of the situation visualized, before looking at the correct answer.

It is a good idea to use a separate sheet of paper for each situation. Divide each page into two columns, like you see in the summary boxes at the end of each chapter. So that you don't miss any important details, write down in the left-hand column all the gestures, movements, positions, and expressions you can see that you think are relevant to the context. Then write down your interpretation of these different elements in the right-hand column. Once you have examined every arm, hand, leg, foot, and facial expression, only then should you write down your conclusion underneath. When making your interpretations, don't forget to apply the five basic principles we discussed in Chapter 1.

Let me introduce you to the method we teach all our students, and depend on for our high-profile interpretations. It's called the SCAN method:

- **SELECT.** Identify and examine one by one the different body language elements that are relevant for the interpretation. Even seemingly neutral elements can sometimes be significant. Check each hand, foot, arm, leg, body position, movement, and facial expression.

- **CALIBRATE.** Apply the five basic principles of body language interpretation from Chapter 1 to each of the selected body language elements. Thoroughly prepare the calibration for the analysis and choice of correct interpretation that you will make in the next step. Reject possible interpretations that do not match the context and examine your final selection critically, in light of each of the five basic principles.

- **ANALYZE.** Reexamine the possible interpretations for the body language elements you have chosen as relevant to the context. Look up the possible meanings for each element in the chapters and summary tables in this book. You will probably have noticed that some of the interpretations are broad and general. In this analytical step, you must try to narrow down the interpretation in relation to the specific context illustrated in the picture.

■ **NOTE.** Write down the relevant elements and interpretations, and then formulate your conclusion. These are three crucial steps that are often overlooked, particularly by beginners. The best way to reach accurate conclusions is to use the two-column approach, listing the body language elements in the left-hand column and their possible interpretations in the right-hand column. Only when you have dealt with all the relevant elements in this manner should you think about drawing up and writing down your conclusions. The more often you do this, the more fluent the process will become, so that you will write shorter and shorter notes.

At the beginning, it is important not to miss any of these steps. If you are interpreting a photograph or film, take all the time you need. If you want to apply the SCAN method during a business conversation, make a SCAN table on the same page as the general notes you are keeping for other aspects of the meeting, perhaps just using a single word for each body language element and interpretation. In this way, you will not only have a record of what was actually said at the meeting, but also a record of its most relevant nonverbal communication. With a bit of practice, you should soon be able to look at your conversation partner and write at the same time. With even more practice, you will eventually begin to note that your brain automatically applies the SCAN method without any need for you to make notes.

This highly effective interpretation method is simple to use. If, after sufficient practice, you apply it correctly, you will soon see every detail of what your conversation partner's body language is expressing, so that you will be able to reach conclusions of remarkable accuracy.

You can now use our SCAN method to interpret the following situations. You can find our interpretations on page 226 and following.

Situation 1

Context: The man on the right has come for a job interview with the two men on the left. Which of the two men is most likely to recommend him for the job?

You can find the answer on page 226.

Situation 2

Context: This is a conversation between colleagues at work. How can you see that the conversation is not going well? Who might be able to put this right?

You can find the answer on page 227.

Situation 3

Context: This is a conversation between a boss and his employees. The boss approaches from the left, the two employees are on the right. It's clear that the boss is unhappy about something. What can we deduce about this situation?

You can find the answer on page 228.

Situation 4

Context: This is a sales conversation. The man on the right is selling a product, the box which is visible on the table. The two men on the left are deciding whether or not buy. The man on the left has an offer in front of him. Will the deal succeed, and what could the salesman do to better his chances?

You can find the answer on page 229.

Answers to the Exercises

Situation 1

Body language elements	Interpretation
Man left: straight back, body	Self-confidence
Man left: hands clasped	Frustration
Man left: right eyebrow raised	Disbelief
Man center: hand alongside face	Assessing with interest
Man right: fingers in pyramid	Self-confidence
Man right: leaning backward	Maintaining distance
Man right: one corner of mouth turned up	Contempt

Conclusion

The man on the right is very sure of himself, as demonstrated by his pyramid hands and superior smile. The man on the left is clearly experiencing frustration, while the man in the middle is more positive. If the man on the left is the boss, the candidate has no chance of getting the job. If the man in the middle is the boss, there is still some hope for the candidate, notwithstanding his arrogant attitude.

Situation 2

Body language elements	Interpretation
Woman left: massaging neck	Frustration
Woman left: looking down	No interest
Woman center: pulling ear	Wants to say something
Woman center: body pointing at man right	Attention for the man
Man right: holding arm behind his back	Controlled frustration
Man right: crossed legs	Closed attitude
Man right: body turned away	Attention elsewhere

Conclusion

The body language of the woman on the left and the man on the right suggests that the conversation is not going well. There is a general atmosphere of frustration. The woman in the middle clearly wants to say something to the man. Perhaps this will improve the situation.

Situation 3

Body language elements	Interpretation
Man left: holding the ball position	Defensiveness
Man left: eyebrows downward and frowning forehead	Self-confidence
Man left: leaning forward	Anger

Situation 3 *(cont.)*

Body language elements	Interpretation
Man left: body directed to man on right	Adds intensity to his anger
Woman middle: hands crossed	Focus is on man on right
Woman middle: hands squeezing her upper arm	Disagreement
Man right: hands in pockets	Controlled anger
Man right: eyebrows upward and wrinkled forehead	Surprise
Man right: body leaned backwards	Surprise and defensiveness

Conclusion

The man on the left is angry about a situation that has occurred. The man on the right seems to be the source of his anger. The woman in the middle doesn't entirely agree with what the man on the left is saying and is resistant to his aggressive approach. The man on the right is surprised by the behavior of the man on the left.

Situation 4

Body language elements	Interpretation
Man right: touching nose	Nervous
Man right: lips stretched in a tense way	Fear

Situation 4 (cont.)

Body language elements	Interpretation
Man middle: avoiding eye contact	Disengaged
Man middle: scratching neck	Light frustration
Man middle: body angled toward middle	Disengaged with person on right
Man left: hand on paper	Reacting to what's on the paper
Man left: hand massaging chin	Thinking
Man left: head downward, white under the eyes	Negative judgement
Man left: leaning back	Lack of interest

Conclusion

The salesman on the right is very nervous which makes him utterly unconvincing. We cannot be sure that he's lying but there is definitely something incongruent about how he presents his product. The potential buyers on the left do not have a positive opinion about the situation. The man on the left definitely has a negative judgement about the product that he is being offered. The man in the middle is disengaged but his reaction is not as negative as the man on the left. The man in the middle is still thinking, but the man on the left has made his decision already, he just hasn't expressed it. This means that if the man on the left is the main decisionmaker, then the salesman has lost. If the man in the middle is the main decisionmaker, then the salesperson still has a chance, but not a good one.

**" Body language signals
are the signposts on your road
to success. "**

Bibliography

Aboyoun, D. C., Dabbs, J. M. (1998). "The Hess Pupil Dilation Findings: Sex or Novelty?" *Social Behavior & Personality* 26(4), 415–419.

Ambady, N., Skowronski, J. J. (2008). *First Impressions.* New York: Guilford Press.

Argyle, M. (1988). *Bodily Communication.* London: Methuen.

Bach, L. (1908). *Pupillenlehre. Anatomie, Physiologie und Pathologie. Methodik der Untersuching.* Berlin: Karger.

Barber, C. (1964). *The Story of Language.* London: Pan Books.

Barton, K., Fugelsang, J., and Smilek, D. (2009). "Inhibiting Beliefs Demands Attention." *Thinking and Reasoning* 15(3), 250–267.

Beebe, S. A. (1979). *Nonverbal Communication in Business: Principles and Applications.*

Bernstein M. J., Young, S. G., Brown, C. M., Sacco D. F., and Claypool, H. M. (1998). "Adaptive Responses to Social Exclusion: Social Rejection Improves Detection of Real and Fake Smiles." *Psychological Science* 19(10), 981–983.

Bernstein M. J., Sacco D. F., Brown, C. M., Young, S. G., and Claypool, H. M. (2010). "A Preference for Genuine Smiles Following Social Exclusion." *Journal of Experimental Social Psychology* 46, 196–199.

Blahna, L. (1975). *A Survey of Research on Sex Differences in Nonverbal Communication.* Speech Communication Association.

Bovée, C. L., Thill, J. V., and Schatzman, B. E. (2003). *Business Communication Today* (7th ed.). New Jersey: Prentice Hall.

Buck, R. (1984). *The Communication of Emotion.* New York: Guilford Press.

Burgoon, J. K., Manusov, V., Mineo, P., Hale, J. L. (1985). "Effects of Gaze on Hiring, Credibility, Attraction and Relational Message Interpretation." *Journal of Nonverbal Behavior* 9(3), 133–146.

Calero, H. H. (2005). *The Power of Nonverbal Communication*. Los Angeles: Silver Lake.

Caputo, J. S., Hazel, H. C., McMahon, C., and Darnels, D. (2002). *Communicating Effectively: Linking Thought and Expression*. Dubuque, Iowa: Kandall-Hunt Publishing.

Carney, D., Cuddy, A. J. C., and Yap, A. (2010). "Power Posing: Brief Nonverbal Displays Affect Neuroendocrine Levels and Risk Tolerance." *Psychological Science* 21(10), 1363–1368.

Chaney, R. H., Linzmayer, L., Grunberger, M., and Saletu, B. (1989). "Pupillary Responses in Recognizing Awareness in Persons with Profound Mental Retardation." *Perceptual & Motor Skills* 69, 523–528.

Cody, M., and O'Hair, D. (1983). "Nonverbal Communication and Deception: Differences in Deception Cues Due to Gender and Communication Dominance." *Communication Monographs* 50, 175–192.

Coker, D. A., and Burgoon, J. K. (1987). "The Nature of Conversational Involvement and Nonverbal Encoding Patterns." *Human Communication Research* 13, 463–494.

Collier, G. (1985). *Emotional Expression*. Hillsdale: Lawrence Erlbaum Associates.

Cuddy, A. J. C., Glick, P., and Beninger, A. (2011). "The Dynamics of Warmth and Competence Judgments, and Their Outcomes in Organizations." *Research in Organizational Behavior* 31, 73–98.

Darwin, C. (1872/1965). *The Expression of the Emotions in Man and Animals*. Chicago: University of Chicago Press.

Davidson, R. J., Scherer, K. R., and Goldsmith, H. H. (2009). *Handbook of Affective Sciences*. New York: Oxford University Press.

Davitz, J. R. (1964). *The Communication of Emotional Meaning*. New York: McGraw-Hill.

DePaulo, B.M., Friedman H. S. (1998). "Nonverbal Communication." In D. Gilbert, S. T. Fiske, and G. Lindzey, eds., *Handbook of Social Psychology* (4th ed.). New York: Random House, 3–40.

Devito, A. J. (2009). *Human Communication*. Boston: Pearson Education.

Di Leo, J. H. (1977). *Child Development: Analysis and Synthesis*. New York: Brunner/Mazel.

Duchenne de Boulogne, C. B. (1862/1990). *The Mechanism of Human Facial Expression*. Cambridge: Cambridge University Press.

Eastwood, J. D., and Smilek, D. (2005). "Functional Consequences of Perceiving Facial Expressions of Emotion Without Awareness." *Consciousness and Cognition* 14(3), 565–584.

Eastwood, J. D., Smilek, D., and Merikle, P.M. (2003). "Negative Facial Expression Captures Attention and Disrupts Performance." *Perception & Psychophysics* 65(3), 352–358.

Ekman, P., Friesen, W. V., and Ellsworth, P. (1972). *Emotions in the Human Face: Guidelines for Research and an Integration of Findings.* New York: Pergamon Press.

Ekman, P. E., Rosenberg, E. L. (1997). *What the Face Reveals; Basic and Applied Studies of Spontaneous Expression Using the Facial Action Coding System.* New York: Oxford University Press.

Exline, R. V., Ellyson, S. L., and Long, B. (1975). "Visual Behavior as an Aspect of Power Role Relationships." In Pliner, Krames, and Alloway (eds.) *Advance.* New York: Plenum, 21–52.

Fast, J. (1991). *Body Language in the Work Place.* New York: Penguin Books.

Feldman, R. S., Rimei, B. (1991). *Fundamentals of Nonverbal Behavior.* Cambridge: Cambridge University Press.

Forbes, R. J., Jackson, P. R. (1980). "Non-verbal Behavior and the Outcome of Selection Interviews." *Journal of Occupational Psychology* 53, 65–72.

Fretz, B. R., Corn, R., Tuemmler, J. M., and Bellet, W. (1979). "Counselor Nonverbal Behaviors and Client Evaluations." *Journal of Counselling Psychology* 26, 304–343.

Friedman, D., Hakerem, G., Sutton, S., and Fleiss, J. L. (1973). "Effect of Stimulus Uncertainty on the Pupillary Dilation Response and the Vertex Evoked Potential." *Electroencephalography and Clinical Neurophysiology* 34, 475–484.

Friedman, H. S., Riggio, R. E. and Casella, D. F. (1988). "Nonverbal Skill, Personal Charisma, and Initial Attraction." *Personality and Social Psychology Bulletin* 74(14), 203–211.

Gilbert, D. T., Fiske, S. T. and Lindzey, G. *The Handbook of Social Psychology* (4th ed., vol. 2). New York: McGraw-Hill, 504–553.

Given, D. B. (2002). *The Nonverbal Dictionary of Gestures, Signs and Body Language Cues.* Washington: Center for Nonverbal Studies Press.

Goode, E. E., Schrof, J. M., and Burke, S. (1998). "Where Emotions Come From." *Psychology* 97/98(62), 54–60.

Goldberg, S., Rosenthal, R. (1986). "Self-touching Behavior in the Job Interview: Antecedents and Consequences." *Journal of Nonverbal Behavior* 10(1), 65–80.

Gunnery, S., Hall, J., and Ruben, M. (2012). "The Deliberate Duchenne Smile: Individual Differences in Expressive Control." *Journal of Nonverbal Behavior.* DOI: 10.1007/s10919-012-0139-4.

Haggard, E. A. and Isaacs, K. S. (1966). "Micro-momentary Facial Expressions as Indicators of Ego Mechanisms in Psychotherapy." In L. A. Gottschalk and A. H. Auerbach (eds.), *Methods of Research in Psychotherapy.* New York: Appleton-Century-Crofts, 154–165.

Hall, E. T. (1973). *The Silent Language.* New York: Anchor.

Hall, E. T. (1976). *The Hidden Dimension*. New York: Doubleday.

Harper, D. (2002). "Talking About Pictures: A Case for Photo Elicitation." *Visual Studies* 17(1), 13–26.

Hertenstein, M. J., Hansel, C. A., Butts A. M., and Hile S. N. (2009). "Smile Intensity in Photographs Predicts Divorce Later in Life." *Motivation and Emotion* 33(2), 99–105.

Hess, E. H. (1964). "Attitude and Pupil Size." *Scientific American* 212, 46–54.

Hess, E. H. (1975). *The Tell-tale Eye: How Your Eyes Reveal Hidden Thoughts and Emotions*. New York: Van Nostrand Reinhold Co.

Hess, E. H., and Polt, J. M. (1960). "Pupil Size as Related to Interest Value of Visual Stimuli." *Science* 132, 349–350.

Hess, E. H., Seltzer, A. L., and Shlien, J. M. (1965). "Pupil Response of Hetero- and Homosexual Males to Pictures of Men and Women: A Pilot Study." *Journal of Abnormal Psychology* 70(3), 165–168.

Hess, U., Kleck, R. (1997). "Differentiating Emotion Elicited and Deliberate Emotional Facial Expressions." *Series in Affective Science*, 271–288.

Hodgins, H., Koestner, R. (1993). "The Origins of Nonverbal Sensitivity." *Personality and Social Psychology Bulletin* 19, 466–473.

Hybels, S., and Weaver, R. L. (2004). *Communicating Effectively*. New York: McGraw-Hill.

Ivy, D. K., and Wahl, S. T. (2008). *The Nonverbal Self: Communication for a Lifetime*. Boston: Allyn & Bacon.

Izard, C. E. (1971). *The Face of Emotion*. East Norwalk, CT: Appleton-Century-Crofts.

Izard, C. E. (1977). *Human Emotions*. New York: Plenum.

Jellison, J. M. (1977). *I'm Sorry, I Didn't Mean To, and Other Lies We Love to Tell*. New York: Chatham Square Press.

Keltner, D., and Bonanno, G. (1997). "A Study of Laughter and Dissociation: Distinct Correlates of Laughter and Smiling During Bereavement." *Journal of Personality and Social Psychology* 73(4), 687–702.

Kleinke, C. L. (1977). "Compliance to Requests Made By Gazing and Touching Experimenters in Field Settings." *Journal of Experimental Social Psychology* 13(3), 218–223.

Knapp, M. L. (1972; 1978). *Nonverbal Communication in Human Interaction*.New York: Holt, Rinehart & Winston.

Knapp, M. L., Hart, R. P., Friedrich, G. W. and Shulma, G. M. (1973). "The Rhetoric of Goodbye: Verbal and Nonverbal Correlates of Human Leave-taking." *Speech Monographs* 40, 182–198.

Kraut, R. E., and Johnston R. E. (1979). "Social and Emotional Messages of Smiling: An Ethological Approach." *Journal of Personality and Social Psychology* 37(9), 1539–1553.

Landis, C. (1924). "Studies of Emotional Reactions II. General Behavior and Facial Expression." *Journal of Comparative Psychology* 4, 447–509.

Levine, A., and Schilder, P. (1942). "The Catatonic Pupil." *The Journal of Nervous and Mental Disease* 96, 1–12.

Littlefield, R. S. (1983). *Competitive Live Discussion: The Effective Use of Nonverbal Cues.* Washington, D.C.: Distributed by ERIC Clearinghouse.

Lock, A. (1993). "Human Language Development and Object Manipulation." In Gibson, K. R. and Ingold, T. (eds.), *Tools, Language, and Cognition in Human Evolution.* Cambridge: Cambridge University Press, 279–310.

Macneilage, P., and Davis, B. (2000). *Evolution of Speech: The Relation Between Ontogeny and Phylogeny.* Cambridge: Cambridge University Press.

Major, B., Schmidlin, A.M., and Williams, L. (1990). "Gender Patterns in Social Touch: The Impact of Setting and Age." *Journal of Personality and Social Psychology* 58, 634–643.

Mann, S., Vrij, A., Nasholm, E., Warmelink, L., Leal, S., and Forrester, D. (2012). "The Direction of Deception: Neuro-linguistic Programming as a Lie Detection Tool." *Journal of Police and Criminal Psychology* 27.

Manusov, V., and Patterson, M., eds. (2006). *The SAGE Handbook of Nonverbal Communication.* Thousand Oaks, CA: Sage Publications.

Mast, M. S., and Hall, J. (2004). "Who Is the Boss and Who Is Not? Accuracy of Judging Status." *Journal of Nonverbal Behavior* 28, 145–165.

McBrearty, S. and Brooks, A. S. (2000). "The Revolution That Wasn't: A New Interpretation of the Origin of Modern Human Behavior." *Journal of Human Evolution* 39, 453–563.

McNeill, D. (2005). *Gesture and Thought.* Chicago: University Of Chicago Press.

McNeill, D., Bertenthal, B., Cole, J., and Gallagher, S. (2005). "Gesture-first, but No Gestures?" *Behavioral and Brain Sciences* 28(2), 138–139.

Mehrabian, A. (1981). *Silent Messages.* Belmont, CA: Wadsworth.

Montepare, J., Koff, E., Zaitchik, D., and Albert, M. (1999). "The Use of Body Movements and Gestures as Cues to Emotions in Younger and Older Adults." *Journal of Nonverbal Behavior* 23, 133–152.

Morris, D., Collett, P., Marsh, P., and O'Shaughnessy, M. (1980). *Gestures: Their Origins and Distribution.* New York: Scarborough.

Nespoulous, J., and Lecours, A. R. (1986). "Gestures: Nature and Function." In J. Nespoulous, P. Perron, and A. R. Lecours (eds.), *Biological Foundations of Gestures: Motor and Semiotic Aspects.* Hillsdale, New Jersey: Lawrence Erlbaum Associates, 49–62.

Neuliep, J. W. (2009). *Intercultural Communication: A Contextual Approach*. Los Angeles: Sage.

Nierenberg, G. I., and Calero, H. H. (2001). *How to Read a Person Like a Book*. New York: Pocket Books.

O'Doherty, J., Winston, J., Critchley, H., Perrett, D., Burt, D. M., and Dolan R. J. (2003). "Beauty in a Smile: The Role of Medial Orbitofrontal Cortex in Facial Attractiveness." *Neuropsychologica* 41(2), 147–155.

O'Hair, D., Cody, M., and McLaughlin, M. (1981). "Prepared Lies, Spontaneous Lies, Machiavellianism, and Nonverbal Communication." *Human Communication Research* 7, 325–339.

Pease, A. (1997). *Body Language: How to Read Other's Thoughts by Their Gestures*. Hampshire, UK: Sheldon Press.

Pease, A., Bease, B. (2004). *The Definite Book of Body Language*. Buderim, Australia: Pease International.

Peters, S. (2012). *The Chimp Paradox: The Acclaimed Mind Management Programme to Help You Achieve Success, Confidence and Happiness*. London: Ebury Publishing.

Plutchik, R. (1980). "A General Psychoevolutionary Theory of Emotion." In R. Plutchik and H. Kellerman (eds.), *Emotion: Theory, Research, and Experience: Vol. 1. Theories of Emotion*. New York: Academic Press, 3–33

Remland, M. S., and Jones, T. S. (1989). "The Effects of Nonverbal Involvement and Communication Apprehension on State Anxiety, Interpersonal Attraction, and Speech Duration." *Communication Quarterly* 37, 170–183.

Richmond, V., McCroskey, J., and Payne, S. (1987). *Nonverbal Behavior in Interpersonal Relationships*. Englewood Cliffs, NJ: Prentice Hall.

Rosenthal R., Hall J. A., DiMatteo, M. R., Rogers, P. L., and Archer, D. (1979). *Sensitivity to Nonverbal Communication: The PONS Test*. Baltimore: Johns Hopkins University Press.

Ruback, R. B., and Hopper, C. H. (1986). "Decision Making by Parole Interviewers: The Effect of Case and Interview Factors." *Law and Human Behavior* 10, 203–214.

Schepartz, L. A. (1993). "Language and Modern Human Origins." *Yearbook of Physical Anthropology* 33, 91–126.

Scher, S., and Rauscher, M. (2003). *Evolutionary Psychology: Alternative Approaches*. New York: Kluwer Press, 2003.

Schlenker, B. R. (1975). "Self-presentation: Managing the Impression Consistency When Reality Interferes with Self-enhancement." *Journal of Personality and Social Psychology* 32, 1030–1037.

Siegman, A. W., and Feldstein, S. (2002). *Nonverbal Behavior and Communication*. Hillsdale, NJ: Erlbaum.

Smilek, D., Eastwood, J. D., Reynolds, M. G., and Kingstone, A. (2007). "Metacognitive Errors in Change Detection: Missing the Gap Between Lab and Life." *Consciousness and Cognition* 16(1), 52–57.

Thill, V. J., and Bovée, L. C. (1999). *Excellence in Business Communication.* New Jersey: Prentice Hall.

Turner, W., and Ortony, A. (1990) "What's Basic about Basic Emotions?" *Psychological Review* 97, 315–331.

Ulbaek, I. (1998). "The Origin of Language and Cognition," (pp. 30–43). In J. R. Hurford, M. Studdert-Kennedy, and C. Knight (eds.), *Approaches to the Evolution of Language.* Cambridge: Cambridge University Press, 30–43.

Wainwright, G. (2003). *Teach Yourself Body Language.* London: Hodder Headline.

Wallace, R. (1989). "Cognitive Mapping and the Origins of Language and Mind." *Current Anthropology* 30, 518–526.

Warmelink, L., Vrij, A., Mann, S., Leal, S., and Poletiek, F. (2011). "The Effects of Unexpected Questions on Detecting Familiar and Unfamiliar Lies." *Psychiatry, Psychology and Law*, 1–7.

Wezowski, K. and Wezowski, P. (2012). *The Micro Expressions Book for Business.* Antwerp: New Vision.

Wezowsk, K. and Wezowski, P. (2012). *How to Reduce Stress with the Emotional Management Method.* Antwerp: New Vision.

Wood, B. S. (1976). *Children and Communication: Verbal and Nonverbal Language Development.* New Jersey: Prentice-Hall.

Yuki, M., Maddux, W. W., and Masuda, T. (2007) "Are the Windows to the Soul the Same in the East and West? Cultural Differences in Using the Eyes and Mouth as Cues to Recognize Emotions in Japan and the United States." *Journal of Experimental Social Psychology* 43, 303–311.

Zuckerman, M., DePaulo, B. M., and Rosenthal, R. (1981). "Verbal and Nonverbal Communication of Deception." In L. Berkowitz (ed.), *Advances in Experimental Social Psychology*, vol. 14. San Diego, CA: Academic Press, 1–59.

Index

acceptance, 122–123
aggression
    arm positions showing, 90
    fists showing, 135–136
    hands placement showing, 105, 204
    index fingers showing, 63–64, 106–108
    reactions to, 81, 116
amazement, 155
analyze (SCAN method), 222
Andrews, Mark A. W., 11
anger
    facial expressions showing, 156
    fists showing, 135–136
    in gestures, 127
    hand position showing, 134
    microexpressions of, 189
ankles, crossed, 114–115
apes, thumb positions in, 61
approval, 39–40
arguing, 73–74
Argyle, M., 169, 171
arms
    crossing of, 19, 88–91, 113, 198
    elbows on chair arm, 202–203
    gestures with barriers of, 95
    partial barrier with, 94–95
arrogance, 61–62, 69–70, 78–80, 110–111
Asian culture, eye contact in, 38
assertiveness, 77–78, 81
assumptions, combinations confirming, 18

Bandler, R. W., 161
Barker, L. L., 170
barriers

as body language reaction, 116
    with hands, 92–93
    through defensive postures, 93–94
    using furniture as, 70–71, 96–97
Bellet, W., 38
Berlusconi, Silvio, 73
BLINK (Body Language Interpretations
        Nominology Know-how) conversation
        technique, 213–216
blinking, 157, 159–160
BMW, 5
bodily tension, 55–56
body language
    changing your, 8–11
    decisionmaking, see decisionmaking
        body language
    intelligence, 1–3, 5–8, 17–23
    negative, see negative body language
    positive, see positive body language
    practice exercises for, 221–229
    self-confident, see self-confident body
        language
    validity of, 11–13
body language intelligence, 1–3, 5–8, 17–23
Body Language Interpretations Nominology
        Know-how (BLINK) conversation
        technique, 213–216
body positions, 40–42, 54–55
boredom, 111
botox, 45
brain, hand gesture effect on, 32
Bulgaria, head nodding in, 122
Buller, D. B., 171
Burgoon, J. K., 45, 161, 170–171

Index

Calero, H. H., 203
calibrate (SCAN method), 222
call centers, body language intelligence in, 5–7
Cassella, D. F., 45
certainty, 75–76, 137
changes, in body language, 20
children, body language affecting, 107
chin, 110–111, 125–126, 194–195
cigarettes, 74–75
"circle" gesture, 22
clearing up, 202
clenched fists, 90
Clinton, Bill, 76, 106
Clinton, Hillary, 3, 41, 76
"Clinton box," 46, 76
clothing, 43–44
Cody, M., 98
Coker, D. A., 45, 170
Coker, R. A., 170
Columbia University, 45
combinations, of movements, 18
communication, extra-linguistic, 99
Condon, William S., 179
confidence, 151, 202–203, *see also* self-confidence
confrontation, 104–105, 113–114, 148–149, 198
contempt, 127, 156, 184–186
context, influencing body language, 19–20
Cook, M., 169
Corn, R., 38
courage, 53
criticism, 108
culture, 22–23, 38, 122

Dalai Lama, 81
Darwin, Charles, 178–179
decisionmaking body language, 193–218
    arm positions in, 198–199, 202–203
    and BLINK conversation techniques, 213–216
    body placements in, 198
    clearing up as, 202
    feet placements in, 199–200
    hand placements in, 194–197, 200–202, 204–207
    head movements in, 200
    indications of lying in, 207–213
    jacket open as, 203
defensiveness, 88, 101–103, 111–115
defensive postures, hidden, 93–94
denial, 109
De Paulo, B. M., 32, 172

disapproval, 104, 123, 157–158
disgust, 127
dislike, 186–188
displeasure, 156
dominance
    and feet wide apart, 71–72
    in handshakes, 67–68
    hands showing, 65–67, 105, 196–198
    index fingers showing, 63–64
    microexpressions of, 186
    and smoking, 74–75
    and thumbs placement, 62
Duchatelet, Roland, 187
Duchenne de Boulogne, Guillaume-Benjamin-Amand, 178
Duchenne smile, 167, 182
Duke University, 45

ego, 59
Ekman, Paul, 179
elbows, 202–203
Ellyson, S. L., 135
emotional intelligence, 5
emotions, displaying, 7–8, 121–143
    after botox, 45
    and decisionmaking, 4
    facial expression, 128
    hand placement, 124–128, 132–136
    head motions, 122–123
    head placement, 130
    leg positions, 137–138
    shoulder placement, 129, 131
    theory of basic, 178
    with upper body, 138–139
    while sitting, 139
    while walking, 140–141
emphasis, through hand movements, 31
equality, handshakes displaying, 33
exercises, practice, 221–229
Exline, R. V., 135
The Expression of Emotions in Man and Animals (Duchenne de Boulogne), 178
expressiveness, 45–46
extra-linguistic communication, 99
eyebrows, 162–165
eye contact
    importance of, 38, 148
    length of, 150–152
    and persuasion, 170
    and self-confidence, 56–57
eyelids, 155, 195
eyes
    closed, 115
    larger, 155

lowering, 128
narrowing, 158–159
and power of persuasion, 169–172
and smiles, 166–168

Facial Action Coding System (FACS), 179
facial expressions, 147–174
    and angry looks, 156
    attentive, 45–46
    blinking in, 157, 159–160
    with eyebrows, 162–165
    eye contact during, 148–152
    and eyelids, 155
    gaze during, 157–158, 160–162
    importance of, 147–148
    persuasion through eyes in, 169–172
    and pupils, 152–154
    real vs. false smiling in, 166–168
    through pursed lips, 165
FACS (Facial Action Coding System), 179
fear
    in gestures, 127
    hand position showing, 126–127, 134
    head position showing, 130
    head scratching showing, 125
    and lying, 210
    microexpressions of, 189
    pupils showing, 153
feet
    direction of, 199–200
    firmly on ground, 137
    stiff, 138
    wide apart, 71–72, 137
finger(s)
    index, 63–64, 106–108, 195
    pressing on pads of, 205–206
    tapping, 99, 136, 205
first impressions, 41–44
fists, 90, 135–136
flirting, and smoking, 74–75
Forbes, R. J., 164
Freisen, Wallace V., 179
Fretz, B. R., 38
Friedman, H. S., 45
Friesen, W. V., 179
frustration, 133, 204
Fujimoto, T., 171
furniture, hiding behind, 96–97

Gallup, Andrew C., 11
Gallup, Gordon G., 11
Gaut, D. A., 170
gaze, averting, 160–162
glance, sideways, 157–158

glasses, in mouth, 195–196
glove handshake, 34–35
Grinder, J., 161

habits, 20–21, 43–44, 70
Haggard, E. A., 178–179
hair, playing with, 124–125
Hale, J. L., 161, 170
Hamm, H. K., 66
hand(s)
    authoritative movements of, 63
    behind head, 197–198
    clasped, 68–70, 91–92, 132
    grasping, 92–93
    against head, 207
    on hips, 62, 80, 105–106
    holding ball with, 58–59
    on knees, 104
    large movements of, 75–76
    left, 34–35
    making pistol with, 204
    open, on table, 31
    palm direction of, 29–30, 65–67
    in pockets, 102–103
    pointing with index finger, 63–64
    pyramids with, 57–58, 78–80, 196–197
    relaxed over each other, 206
    rubbing, 132–133, 205
    shaky, 134
    on side of face, 200–201
    stiff, 135
    stop signal with, 103
    talking with your, 32
    thumbs up with, 59
    toward mouth, 97
handshake(s), 32–35, 67–68
happiness, 127, 181–185
Harper, D., 169
Harper, R. G., 169
Havas, David, 45
head
    dropping, and tensed shoulders, 109–110
    hands against, 207
    lowered with puzzled expression, 108
    moving back, with neck rigid, 109
    nodding your, 39, 122–123
    raising, to horizontal, 110
    scratching your, 125
    shaking no with, 123
    between shoulders, 98–99, 130
    supporting the, 111, 201–202
    tilting of, 36–37
    turning away, 100–101
Hess, Eckhard, 152

Index

hidden defensive postures, 93–94
"holding the ball," 58–59
Hopper, C. H., 92
human touch, persuasive power of, 66–67

impressions, first, 41–44
incongruencies, to establish lies, 211
independence, 75–76
index finger, 63–64, 106–108, 195
insecurity, 94–97, 109–110, 125–126,
    139
intelligence, emotional, 5
intentions, 29–30, 37–38
interest
    eyes showing, 115
    hand positions showing, 200–201
    head position showing, 36–37
    legs positions showing, 35–36
    pupils showing, 153–154
    sexual, 60–62, 148–149
    shoulders showing, 129
    upper body showing, 28–29, 100–101,
        138–139, 198
    wrists showing, 134–135
International Conference on Yawning, 11
interviews, 55, 101, 224, 226
irritation, 131, 136
Isaacs, K. S., 178–179

jacket, open, 203
Jackson, P. R., 164
James Bond (film), 54
Japan, head nodding in, 122
jaw, highly mobile, 54
Jobs, Steve, 58–59
Jones, T. S., 122
joy, smile of, 182

Kerk, Kleine, 169
Kleinke, C. L., 66

Leal, Sharon, 159
Leathers, D. G., 56
left hand, implications of, 34–35
legs
    crossing, 73, 111–113
    horizontal at 90 degrees, 113–114
    stiff, 138
    stretching out, 35–36, 74, 104–105
    wide apart, 137
limbic system, 18–19
lips, 165, 188, 195
listening, 39, 122–123

Long, B., 135
lying, indications of, 207–213

Macron, Emmanuel, 34
Major, B., 66
Malandro, L. A., 170
Manusov, V., 161, 170
marriage, 10–11
Matarazzo, J. D., 169
McLaughlin, M., 98
Mehrabian, A., 171–172
men, 33–34, 66, 72
microexpressions, 177–190
    contempt in, 185–186
    and culture, 22
    defined, 177–180
    dislike in, 186–188
    fear/anger/sadness/surprise in, 189
    happiness in, 181–185
    importance of, 4
    recognizing, 183
    using neutral face for, 180–181
Middle Ages, 122
Middle East, handshakes in, 33
millionaires, microexpressions of, 187–188
Mineo, P., 161, 170
mirroring, 39–40
Morris, Desmond, 12
motivation, and slouching, 129
mouth
    covering, 97–98, 126–127
    fingers/objects in, 98, 124, 196
    hand movements near, 31
movements, words vs., 18–19
movies, Western, 61
Myo Company, 4–5

NATO conference (2017), 34
neck, rubbing back of, 204
negative body language, 87–118
    arm positions in, 88–91, 94–95
    during decisionmaking process, 201
    facial expressions in, 115
    hand positions in, 91–93, 97–99,
        101–108
    head positions in, 98–100, 108–111
    and hidden defensive postures, 93–94
    and hiding, 96–97
    leg positions in, 104–105, 111–115
    reacting to, 116–117
negotiations, 4, 36–37, 151, 193
nervousness
    fingers showing, 99

hand position showing, 91–92, 134, 205
  leg position showing, 111–113
  partial arm barrier showing, 94–95
Neuro-Linguistic Programming (NLP), 161–162
neutral face, 180–181
newborns, 148
Nierenberg, G. I., 203
Nixon, Richard, 106
NLP (Neuro-Linguistic Programming), 161–162
nodding, 122–123, 199, 200
note (SCAN method), 223

Obama, Barack, 2–3, 37, 41
O'Hair, D., 98
opened palms, 29–30
openness
  hand gestures showing, 29–30, 31
  open jacket showing, 203
  shoulders showing, 129
  wrists showing, 30, 134–135
orbicularis oculi, 166–167

pain, 13
palms, opened, 29–30
personal space, and handshakes, 35
persuasion, 169–172
"the pistol," 204
Plutchik, Robert, 178
poker face, 181
politicians, index fingers of, 106
Portsmouth University, 159
positive body language, 51–83
  arrogance vs., 78–80
  and assertiveness signals, 77–78, 81
  facial expressions showing, 54, 56–57
  hand placements in, 57–70, 75–76
  leg positions in, 71–74
  and relaxation, 55–56
  shoulder positions in, 53
  and smoking, 74–75
  in upper body, 54–55
  while sitting, 70–71
  winner's pose as, 52–53
power, 66, 68–69
power positions, see self-confident body language
practice exercises, 221–229
presentations, 41–44
presidential elections, U.S., 2–3, 41–42
pressure, during handshakes, 33–34
pupils, of eyes, 152–154

rational thought, 18–19
refusal, 198
rejection, 103, 109
relationships, body language in, 10–11
relaxation
  and body language, 9
  body positions showing, 41–42
  hands showing, 102–103, 206
  of jaw, 54
  as sign of control, 55–56
  while walking, 141
Remland, M. S., 122
repetition, 18
resistance, 111–113
respect, 38, 60
Riggio, R. E., 45
right hand, 125
Roman times, 32, 59
Romney, Mitt, 2–3, 41–42
Rosenthal, R., 32, 172
Ruback, R. B., 92
Ruch, Willibard, 168

sadness, 128, 189
Saine, T., 170
salespeople, 4, 225, 228–229
SCAN method, 222–223
Schmidlin, A. M., 66
select (SCAN method), 222
self-confidence, 52–53, 137
self-confident body language, 27–47
  body positioning for, 40–42
  example of, 27
  facial expressions for, 37–38, 45–46
  habits and clothing in, 43–44
  hand positions in, 29–35
  head movements for, 36–37, 39
  leg positions in, 35–36
  mirroring to show, 39–40
  in upper body, 28–29
self-control, 133
sexual interest, 60–62, 148–149
shoulders
  back, 129
  head between, 98–99, 130
  relaxed, 53
  sagging, 131
  shrugging, 131
shyness, 12–13
  eyes showing, 128, 150
  gestures with arm barriers showing, 95
  and playing with hair, 124–125
sideways glance, 157–158

sitting, 31, 70–71, 139
slouching, 129
smile, 37–38, 166–168, 182, 186
Smilek, Daniel, 159
smoking, 74–75
staring, 148–149
status, hand position showing, 68–69
stress, 135
stubbornness, 91
success, 1–3
superiority, 156
surprise, 128, 162, 189

tense positions, 90–91, 135
tension, bodily, 55–56
thought, rational, 18–19
threats, head responses to, 98–99
thumbs
    behind your belt, 61–62
    holding your own, 101–102
    outside your pockets, 60, 80
    pointing with your, 60
    up, with arms crossed, 62
    up vs. down, 59
Time magazine, 101
timing, importance of, 20
touch, human, 66–67
training, 8–9, 221–229
Trump, Donald, 3, 34
trust, 29, 34–35, 76
Tuemmler, J. M., 38

uncertainty
    eyes showing, 128, 150
    hand placement showing, 124, 126–127
    thumb showing, 101–102
understanding, tilting head showing,
        36–37
unease, 132, 140
University of Southern California, 45

University of Wisconsin-Madison, 45
upper body
    leaning forward vs. backward with,
        28–29, 40, 198
    showing attention with, 138
    turning away, 100–101, 139
U.S. presidential elections, 2–3, 41–42

vulnerability, 36–37

walking, 140–141
warnings, 63–64
weakness, 131
Webbink, P., 171
Western culture, 38, 122
Western movies, 61
Wiens, A. N., 169
Williams, L., 66
Willis, F. N., 66
Winfrey, Oprah, 101
winking, 157
winner's pose, 52–53
withdrawal, 138
women
    defensive postures in, 93–94
    displaying thumbs by, 60
    handshakes with, 33–34
    human touch in, 66
    leg crossing in, 112–113
    playing with hair by, 124–125
Woodall, W. G., 171
words, movements vs., 18–19
workplace, body language in, 224–229
wrinkles, 188
wrists, 30, 133–135

yawning, 11

Zuckerman, M., 32
zygomatic major, 166–167